message me

message me

listening for God in our relationships

Kemper and Laura Lewis

TATE PUBLISHING
AND ENTERPRISES, LLC

Published by Tate Publishing & Enterprises, LLC
127 E. Trade Center Terrace | Mustang, Oklahoma 73064 USA
1.888.361.9473 | www.tatepublishing.com

Tate Publishing is committed to excellence in the publishing industry. The company reflects the philosophy established by the founders, based on Psalm 68:11,
"The Lord gave the word and great was the company of those who published it."

Book design copyright © 2014 by Tate Publishing, LLC. All rights reserved.
Cover design by Junriel Boquecosa
Interior design by Jimmy Sevilleno

Published in the United States of America

ISBN: 978-1-63063-134-5
1. Family & Relationships / Love & Romance
2. Family & Relationships / General
14.03.17

DEDICATION

TO THE VICTIMS of sex trafficking and to those who war against it.

To Jesus Christ, the one who has authored our faith and will be faithful to complete it.

ACKNOWLEDGMENTS

WE ARE GRATEFUL to every person who sent us an email, hoping to be directed to truth in the midst of their circumstances. Although you remain anonymous for the protection of others, our God surely knows you and he will bless your courage.

We would like to thank our friends Wes and Connie Aarum, who, together, followed God's direction and began the Vintage ministry in 1998. Through your obedience to God's Word, many lives, including our own, "have turned to God from idols, to serve the living God" (1 Thessalonians 1:9). We could not be more grateful.

To Pastor Jerry Gillis, thank you for having the visionary leadership to invest in young adults.

We would like to thank Tate Publishers for partnering with us to support Agape International with this project.

Thank you Jaime Snyder and Tami Paycheck for bringing joy and organization to piles of paper and a dream.

Thank you John Gannon for your valuable feedback and time.

Thank you Rebekah Ruth, Lisa Littlewood, Christen Civiletto Morris, Kelly Baesen, and Marissa Albrecht for sharing your God-given creativity and inspirational skills.

Thank you to our friend Laura Stenman, who not only introduced us but also continued to ask, "Have you finished the book yet?"

We are grateful to our family who are a daily reminder that love protects.

To our children, Kamryn and Kaden, it is our hope that the truth revealed in God's Word about relationships will purify and guard your hearts and minds in Christ Jesus.

CONTENTS

PREFACE

WHAT DAY IS it today in your life? For us it is June 22, 2012. We are excited that we get to meet you—in your life, on this day—whatever day it is for you! Together we are beginning a journey, hand in hand and heart to heart, through the Word of God! How exciting is that?

We are flipping out that you have chosen to walk with God, and that we get to be a part of your conversations with him through this book. Thank you for that privilege. Please know that this time with you is a gift to our lives, and we are praying for you with huge faith that we will learn much together with our God.

This book is a long-awaited hope of ours. If you are holding it, know you are holding an answer to our prayers for all of us! That your life and our lives, and the lives of several other people you will get to meet as you read, would actually intersect on the pages of this book is something only God could do!

As you read this journal, we pray that you will see in full color the wonders of God's spirit at work in the hearts of young men and women—just like you—who have longed for God and cried out for his help. They have chosen to be bold and honest with their mistakes, their heartache, their learning, and their hope in God.

Since 1998, we have served in college ministry at The Chapel at CrossPoint in Buffalo, New York, and have had the joy of hearing many young adults share their dating and relationship stories and their fight for sexual purity. Their letters to us have been recorded here anonymously so that you may hear the truth of God concerning your own heart, mind, and body and find victory with these letter writers in Christ.

Pack your suitcase for this journey. This book will be our main connection to one another, but as we travel together with Jesus, please pack some other important tools with you. You're going to need a study Bible. If you don't have one, invest in one. If you can't afford one right now, Crosswalk.com or Biblegateway.com will be a big help to you. The purpose of this book is to connect you to God and to connect you to other people seeking God. If you don't have your Bible open as we all talk and think together, you'll miss out on the most important part of the conversation—God's Word!

You'll need a pen. Every time you come together with us, you can write on the pages of this book. Write down your thoughts, questions, your own personal examples, prayers, and the truth God is making clear to you. Writing is a learning tool, for you and for us, and as you will see, it has been a tool for those who have written to us. What would we have to share if they had not written to us? Greater still, what would we have to share if God had not written to us? Find the words to match the lessons of your heart, mind, and body and then write them down so you can actually see your thoughts take formation. Read those personal thoughts out loud to yourself, and share them with someone else.

Those carefully considered lessons should spring you into action to transform your life into one that will bring glory to our God and great joy to your soul.

INTRODUCTION

OUR **INTIMATE CONNECTION** to God is critical to every connection we have with others.

Relationships matter. Consider God's amazing design for the pulse of life. A heart is attached to everything you are, everything you say, and everything you do. The heart of God and the heart of another human being are connected to your life, your words, and your actions, including those words and actions you withhold and those you choose to practice alone. Every part of you impacts all of us. This is a huge life concept—God-sized in design and purpose.

The Son of God taught us,

> As the Father has loved me, so I have loved you. Now remain in my love. If you keep my commands you will remain in my love, just as I have kept my Father's commands and remain in his love. I have told you this so that my joy may be in you and that your joy may be complete. My command is this: love each other as I have loved you (John 15:9-12).

Relationships indeed matter to our Savior—to our God. "Greater love has no one than this: to lay down one's life for one's friends" (John 15:13). Great love requires a sacrifice, not a sacrifice we choose, but rather one we were given to lay down for others.

Seeking God's instruction and help in our relationship with him and with others would be wise then, wouldn't it? Think about this: he is the provider of life and love, and he has abundantly provided. We are blessed with everything we need so that we can love him and love others well. Everything we need? Yes everything! Please read and study 2 Peter 1:1–11. Will you seriously and wholeheartedly take a moment to read through these verses to figure out what you can do to love God and others well? Why wouldn't you, right? We should be flipping out over this opportunity—and not only flipping out while running for our copy of God's Word, but also encouraging and helping one another to do the same thing. So, are you running for your Bible?

Our abundant life and joy in relationships is possible through the living Word of God. If we—Kemper and Laura—would have only realized this truth when we were younger, many regrets and scars could have been spared. Regret is a harsh teacher. Jesus is not. His teachings are easy and light. And his living Word—active in us—will bless us in our relationships, protect us from evil, and perfectly provide for us as his children. Hear our hearts in this moment that are beating to be connected to yours. By the Holy Spirit, we—all of us—ache for the love of God, and we long for others to know his love as well. What a miracle! This is God's Word, faithful and true. Our prayer is that together we grasp the truth that relationships matter, and for his glory, pass it on in all we are, in all we say and do, in all we refrain from saying, and in all we refrain from doing. This is love; this is great love.

LISTEN: THE POSITION OF OUR HEART

Jesus said, "My sheep listen to my voice; I know them, and they follow me" (John 10:27). God has spoken. His Word is a gift to hear, receive, and live every single day. The question is: are we listening? Do we turn off the static that is often our own voice, so that we can listen to God? Do we focus on the Word of God so that we see how it revolves around him, or do we try to make it revolve around us? Do we look to receive a message from God, or do we try to write our own message as our circumstances dictate?

Because of Jesus, we have been given everything we need to be in constant communication with our God. We have been given a new heart that aches for his Word. We have the Holy Spirit to teach us all the things we need to know. We have access to the God of the universe, all frequencies open and paid for. What amazing grace! But in our communication with God, who is the one doing all the talking?

Every aspect of our created need for God is met in God and so we pray; we sing; we call out for his attention to our lives. And the beautiful truth is he knows what we need before we utter one syllable. God listens to us, but do we listen to him? This is not just about hearing God, because listening is different. Listening is hearing with intention. Do we intentionally listen to God?

We should then consider very carefully that Jesus said, "My sheep listen to my voice" (John 10:27a). His voice is his Word. How do we—those of us who claim to be his followers—listen to his Word? Jesus modeled what listening to the Word of God looks like.

> As the Father has loved me, so have I loved you. Now remain in my love. If you keep my commands, you will remain in my love, just as I have kept my Father's commands and remain in his love. I have told you this so that my joy may be in you and that your joy may be complete.
>
> John 15:9-11

Jesus's relationship with the Father was to demonstrate love for him by the way he kept his Word. It is the same for us.

Every aspect of our relationship to God flows out of his Word. To keep his commands, we need to know his Word. By doing so, we will ultimately learn who he is. And when we know our God, we will trust his commands. As we follow his Word by living out his commands, we will realize the abiding love that Jesus died for us to experience. And in this complete joy we will continue to listen with great intensity to his voice, over every other voice, even our own.

Jesus taught us that listening to the voice of God is critical as his people, and he modeled for us that obedience to his Word is absolutely everything. We must study to hear his voice and follow his lead. Only then can joy be assured.

STUDY: THE POSITION OF OUR MIND

A gift of God to the believer is a heart that actually desires him. Being a part of a church body is where we can fully express that desire to learn, grow, and worship with others. However, if this is the only time we connect with God, who then are we actually following? The time we spend with God in prayer and personal Bible study is critical to who we are as his followers. What do you think we should value more, getting a text message directly from our Creator and Savior, or hearing everyone around us always talking about the message that he sent to them? Even if our friends let us read what God said to them, it's just not the same. It's not the one-on-one intimacy we crave.

We go to some pretty pricy measures to be connected to our friends, don't we? If you own a cell phone, you obviously want to be reached. Every message represents a relationship and one that is your personal privilege. So when you send a text message, don't you wait to get one in return? And don't you read the reply as soon as you can? What if you never received a reply? Or what if you received the reply, but it had nothing to do with your text? Wouldn't you feel a giant disconnect?

Being connected plays a critical role in our relationships. Are you tracking with us here? We have the opportunity to connect one-on-one with God. There's no delay on that incoming message either. His Word is waiting for us right now! And by his Holy Spirit—who is all about our immediate connection—we can read and understand what God has said. And what is even more mind-blowing is that our God will speak specifically into our personal lives, and he cares about our reply!

Why do we let anything stop us from the Word of God? God wrote to us so we that we could know him. In fact we were created not only to hear, know, and receive his Word with a willing heart, but also to reflect the message of God and bring him glory as we live it! Doesn't that just make you want to pound something? Pound your heart, my friend! That's the Spirit of God in you!

When Howard Hendricks, a long-time professor at Dallas Theological Seminary (who also served as the Dallas Cowboys chaplain from 1976 to 1984), spoke about personal Bible study, he put it simply, "There is no jewel more precious than the one which you have mined yourself." Dig into God's Word for yourself! The work is part of the gift.

Some effective Bible study methods are provided for you to consider using in your study time with God. These are questions and reading strategies geared toward slowing down our thinking to a meditative pace. And the goal of each strategy is the same: accurate interpretation and personal application. Ask God the same thing the psalmist asked, "Open my eyes that I may see wonderful things from your law" (Psalm 119:18).

Prepare to study God's Word:

1. Schedule your Bible study time into your day.

2. Keep a notebook.

3. Get the right tools.

4. Spend time in prayer before you study.

Use study tools:

1. A study Bible (NIV and NASB offer concordances)

2. A Bible dictionary and/or Bible encyclopedia

3. An exhaustive concordance (e.g., Strong's NIV or NASB Exhaustive Concordance from Zondervan)

SUGGESTED STUDY METHODS

The Vintage method is question driven (Vintagetruth.com).

1. Pray for insight on how to apply the passage of Scripture you have studied.

2. Meditate on the verse(s) you have chosen to study.

3. Write out what you understood from the passage and then write out a plan of application.

    a. Is there a sin to confess?

    b. Is there a promise to claim?

    c. Is there an attitude to change?

    d. Is there a command to obey?

    e. Is there an example to follow? Or is there a positive one to copy or a negative one to avoid?

    f. Is there a prayer to pray?

    g. Is there an error to avoid?

    h. Is there a truth to believe?

    i. Is there something to praise God for?

4. Memorize a key verse from your study.

The In and Through Method is application driven.

1. Pray for insight about the passage of Scripture you are about to study.

2. In your journal, make two columns the length of the page. Label one "In" and the other "Through."

3. Read the passage several times.

4. Then, under the "In" column, write out, using exact words from the text, the truths you learned from that passage. These are the facts that will guide your beliefs and choices as you live in Christ.

5. With any lesson, there should be application. The "Through" column is where you will write out the actions that will come through your life in response to what you have learned from the passage and noted under the "In" column.

To consider the impact these truths have on your personal relationship to Christ, there are a few questions you should ask yourself:

1. What truth have I just learned? Write the facts you read in the passage under the "In" column. And then, in light of that understanding, ask yourself:

2. How will that truth come through my life? Here are some examples:

   a. In your thoughts, "I now understand…"

   b. In your actions, "I will do…"

   c. In your words, "I will say…"

d. In your character, "I will be…"

e. In defining your beliefs about God, "I believe God is…"

f. In defining your beliefs about the Bible, "I have learned the Bible is…"

g. In defining your relationship with Christ, "Jesus is…"

h. In defining your relationship with others, "In my relationships, I will…"

Write your life action in response to God's Word under the "Through" column on your journal paper. For example, the verse is "Jesus replied, anyone who loves me will obey my teaching" (John 14:23). Here's a look at what you could write in your journal:

IN	THROUGH
v. 23 Anyone who loves Jesus obeys what he says.	To demonstrate my love for Jesus, I will obey what he says.

The Precept Method (*How to Study the Bible* by Kay Arthur) is an in depth study approach.

1. Read the passage several times.

2. Read with purpose (to know a character, a truth, a promise, a topic, a theme, a chapter, a word).

3. Observe the obvious facts: type of book, author, audience, people, places, repeated words, setting, and events.

4. Identify the context (words, phrases, and sentences surrounding a particular word, phrase, or sentence).

    a. Context is king! Identify details given before and after the passage as well as within the passage.

    b. Ask hard questions that will make you dig.

i. Ask who, what, where, when, why, and how.

ii. Identify key people, events, words, and phrases.

iii. What type of book are you in (e.g., historical, biographical, poetic, proverbial, prophetic, epistle, combination)?

5. Consider all of the details given in the text, and do not infer without fact (specific words, contrasts, comparisons, expressions of time, evidence of the culture, and quoted Scripture).

6. Deal with the text objectively (let the text speak for itself).

   a. Read the conversation carefully.

   b. Read words and actions with insight into the characters, the events, the culture, and the entire context.

7. Cross-reference (e.g., Biblestudytools.com).

8. Compare translations (e.g., Crosswalk.com).

9. Write down what you learn from each passage you study.

Before you interpret, keep the following in mind:

1. Context is king in interpretation; it rules.

2. Be careful not to contradict the general theme of the book you are studying.

3. Look for the author's intended meaning of the passage.

4. Check to be sure your conclusions are in accordance or agreement with what the author said in other books of his writing.

5. Make sure your conclusions do not violate other biblical truths. Scripture will never contradict Scripture.

Lastly, focus on the application in your life:

1. Pray for insight on how to apply the passage of Scripture you have studied.

2. Write out your personal application plan. For example:

Based on:

I am going to:

3. How will you evaluate the transformation of your life?

FROM THIS POINT FORWARD

THE LETTER ENTRIES that follow are all real letters that we have received from college-aged young adults. Specific names and details have been changed to protect the privacy of our friends and their families.

We hope that as you read about their relationship struggles and the truth that heals them, you will be strengthened and more determined to live for God. Examine their circumstances with God's Word, so that he can help you see him through your own.

After each message there is a section provided for you to pause and personally study the Scripture mentioned.

Selected Scripture:

Study method:

Truth learned:

Steps I will take to apply it:

My message concerning this letter:

This section is an opportunity for you to join the conversation. *Message Me* is our heart, soul, mind and body lessons welded together with the Word of God.

The bulk of your study should be recorded in your personal journal or notebook so you have a reminder of the places God took you in your heart and in his Word. You will want to remember each verse so you can retrace your steps, memorize them if you are so inclined, share this biblical journey with others, or just look back and be amazed at the faithfulness of God to speak to you so clearly.

Consider, also, that many of you will be moms or dads someday, and some of you may be moms and dads now. Your journal or notebook will become part of your legacy to your kids as they get to learn from your victories, your defeats, and how God faithfully taught you truth in the midst of both.

We cannot live or love with full joy apart from God's Word. So, *with strong resolve*, look for the proof of that statement as you read letter after letter. Examine each question and reply closely. Then *consider* your own life, your relationships, and what God is showing you with regard to your relationships. Go directly to the *Scripture* that is given *and ask God* what he would have you learn. Invest your heart and mind and body in this journey with us, or you will miss the purpose of this book, which is *to personally message you*!

See the italicized text in the preceding paragraph? Go back and read just the italicized script. There was a message hidden there for you in plain sight. Did you find it? There is always more to consider than just what is written in plain black and white. Ask God to open your eyes to what he wants you to see and understand. Be diligent. He will do it. This is his will for you and us.

> Open my eyes that I may see wonderful things from your law.
>
> Psalm 119:18

> Give me understanding, so that I may keep your law and obey it with all my heart.
>
> Psalm 119:34

Friends, this resource was written over years, miles, and cyberspace, by broken hearts and yielded minds, to help you know and love Christ more deeply. In him are all the treasures of wisdom and knowledge. Set your heart and mind on Christ. He will guide you in all truth. We are hoping in him for you!

> Being strengthened with all power according to his glorious might so that you may have great endurance and patience, and giving joyful thanks to the Father, who has qualified you to share in the inheritance of his people in the kingdom of light.
>
> Colossians 1:11-12

LETTERS BETWEEN WOMEN OF GOD

IT IS MY privilege to share the dialogue that I have had with women seeking God over years of college ministry. Like a biblical character we read of and learn from, our God has introduced us to these young women to learn of his powerful life-changing truth. Their reason for writing and making their letters public was to bring to light the truth of God's Word in the midst of their circumstances. When they wrote to me, they thought of you. Although their names are not mentioned, and you and I do not get to see the details of their faces, we get to know their heart for God—which is the most beautiful thing about every woman. I pray you see the glory of God in each life, and in personal reflection, realize his glory in your own.

Love,
Laura

A SINGLE PORTION

DEAR LAURA,
I know that the Bible says that this is the best time of my life. As a single girl, I have freedom I will never have again. But I watch others my age who have found the one for them, and I have yet to date anyone. Why can't I just shut off the part of my head that says I have to be in a relationship now?

Reply:

Hi! Thanks for writing! I am grateful to hear from you and for this opportunity to learn with you. Your words have gripped my heart because they reflect yours. I want to encourage you with what God has to say, because my words and my thoughts, even though I care very much for where you are and what you are feeling, they would fail in comparison to the love, and hope, and truth of God's Word.

I want you to consider with me the first statement in your message. You said, "I know that the Bible says that this is the best time of my life." I think you have stated part of the truth—but not the whole truth. This time in your life is like every other time in your life that you have lived and yet to live—it is purposed by God. In Psalm 139:16 the Psalmist says, "all the days ordained for me were written in your book before one of them came to be." Not one day is unintended, and that truth alone stirs my heart when I wake up to pursue God in each day.

That thought didn't used to move me. I used to wake and get up to live for myself, until God taught me who he was and what I was missing in my empty pursuits of satisfaction. Every day is a day of purpose that God ordained. How you view it does not determine its value. It is of God that you should live and breathe. Where you are in your singleness today, sweet one, is in an opportunity to live in undivided devotion to God. Paul instructed the Corinthians in this truth in 1 Corinthians 7. Check it out when you get a chance, but I would like to highlight a few verses for us. In 1 Corinthians 7:17 it says concerning married life and single life, "Nevertheless, each of you should live as a believer in whatever situation the Lord has assigned to you, just as God has called you." Wow! So much from that one verse speaks volumes.

Are you hearing truth with me? Live as a believer in whatever situation the Lord has assigned. As a believer, how do we live? That is a great question, and one that should send us on a life-long pursuit through God's Word. The whole Bible speaks to that. We live in obedience to God—loving him with all our heart, soul, mind, and strength (Mark 12:29-30). And, wow, expressing that will take our entire lives, right? And the part of that verse that says, "in whatever situation the Lord has assigned"—now there's some truth we need to soak up. This time of your life is assigned by God. He gave you this specific time in your life and assigned it to you in his book before you took your first breath. To absorb that truth, pray about it, and seek God daily in light of that truth. Seeking God for what is actually true is where peace and joy can be found. God's Word is our perspective adjuster day in and day out. My heart, although I ache to be steadfast moment by moment, is prone to wander, and so it deceives me. Every day—as God's mercies are new for us—again we need to seek his perspective to embrace him as we live in the day he made for his purposes.

Consider with me what Paul writes to women in their singleness:

> An unmarried woman or virgin is concerned about the Lord's affairs: Her aim is to be devoted to the Lord in both body and spirit. But a married woman is concerned about the affairs of this world—how she can please her husband. I am saying this for your own good, not to restrict you, but that you may live in a right way in undivided devotion to the Lord.
>
> 1 Corinthians 7:34b-35

Now, here's where your first statement comes in. You can choose to see this as the best time of your life, or not. It's up to you. The joy is there if you choose to find it. Jesus promised that he brought life to the fullest. Will we choose to live in that truth or lament over our circumstances? Paul rejoiced in his circumstances—not because they always felt good—but because he chose to live out of the truth that his days were of God for his glory through Paul. Everything in his life he surrendered to God for one purpose: the sake of the Gospel of Jesus Christ. Check out 1 Corinthians 9:19-23. Whether you are single and learning to be devoted to the Lord, or married and learning to be devoted to the Lord in your marriage, both are purposed for the glory of God through Christ.

You may not feel like it is a hootin' and hollerin' party in the moment. But feelings have very little to do with this life in Christ. In fact, the one thing I have learned about my feelings is that I must surrender them to God—in my joy, in my sorrow, in my longing, and in my satisfaction, my feelings are also to be surrendered to God. Feelings can be so deceptive, and God would not have given them to us, unless they, too, were ours to give back to him. We as believers are a people who surrender to God—in everything. See Proverbs 3:5-6.

Will you read 1 Corinthians when you get a chance? And may I encourage you to read Psalm 119 as well? So much goodness in God's Word! Enjoy it every day!

Psalm 119:57 says, "You are my portion, Lord." What does the Psalmist mean by that? Portion of what? Food? Goodness? Joy? Love? Sorrow? Pain? Life? What is a God portion? All of him? Some of him? How does he know what I need? Why do others seem to have more? Lots of questions to consider. What does it mean, my friend, that God is our portion? Don't you wonder why God would make that statement live in his Word? I did. I wondered big time, and I sought the meaning of that powerful truth at a time in my life when I wasn't single, but married with two babies at my feet.

Circumstances—even when they are full of blessing—will never satisfy you. God is the only one who will ever be your portion. And it is good to be satisfied by him and him alone. We need to know who he is, really know him, or we won't realize the fullness—and goodness—of the portion that is ours. Then, everything else—everything and everyone else—will rest well in your heart, soul, mind and strength with correct perspective as God intended those people and circumstances for you. He intended them, my friend, before you were even a life with a heart to beat and long for him. Read Psalm 119 carefully and prayerfully and ask God what it means that he is your portion.

Thank you for trusting me with your heart. I have prayed about this opportunity, and am hopeful that this note brings you encouragement. Please be sure to examine my words pressed up tight with what God has said in his: 1 Corinthians 7 and Psalm 119.

> Yet I am always with you; you hold me by my right hand. You guide me with your counsel, and afterward you will take me into glory. Who have I in heaven but you? And earth has nothing I desire besides you. My flesh and my

heart may fail, but God is the strength of my heart and my portion forever.

Psalm 73:23-26

Love,
Laura

PERSONAL STUDY

You ready to jump into the conversation? Please use the scripture mentioned in this message, and take some time on your own to hear from our God. You'll need your Bible, journal or notebook, a pen, and an open heart to hear what God has to say to you today. Choose a study method to guide your thinking, pray before you begin, and ask God for a message from him that is specific to your heart, your needs, and the questions that his spirit is drawing you to ask.

Selected Scripture:

Study method:

Truth learned:

Steps I will take to apply it:

My message concerning "A Single Portion":

BE SURE IT'S TRUE

DEAR LAURA,
I've been dating a wonderful guy for about six months now. He loves God, treats me right, and we have an awesome relationship. But he hasn't said those three little magic words, "I love you" yet. I know that I shouldn't say it first, but people are telling me that he should have said it by now, and that I need to talk to him about it. He's naturally a "think first, act later" kind of guy, so I've never really worried until people started talking to me about it. Should I be concerned that he hasn't?

Reply:
So, this special guy hasn't said that he loves you, huh? Well, actually, I think that's very wise on his part. This is one of those times where I look at the rule by which we are basing our reasoning and actions and go: "hmmmmm...." I mean, think about it. Who told you that time was the determining factor for when those powerful words should be spoken into your relationship? Time is not the factor at all. Investing time in the relationship to get to know each other is wise, but that time, whether 6 months or a year, is not the factor that should determine when you say "I love you". Love is a choice, one that requires great sacrifice from the man who is brave enough to embrace such a commitment to you.

Check out this verse:

> Husbands, love your wives, just as Christ loved the church and gave himself up for her to make her holy, cleansing her by the washing with water through the word, and to present her to himself as a radiant church without stain or wrinkle or any other blemish, but holy and blameless.
>
> Ephesians 5:25-27

Paul goes on to teach that husbands are to love their wives as their own bodies. Wow! What a commitment this young man will choose one day! What a huge responsibility for the rest of his life! Would you really want your boyfriend to say "I love you" if this commitment were not at the core of what he was saying? If this commitment were not attached to his words, what would he really be saying if he said "I love you"? That's a scary thought. Can't he communicate his interest in you and his attraction to you in other ways and in other words that may one day define more clearly the basis of his love? Words like:

- You're really pretty.
- You are fun to be around.
- You make me laugh.
- You encourage me.
- You help me think about life in a new way.
- You help me love God better.
- You help me want to live like a godly man.
- You have changed me for the better.
- You are so good to me.
- You are interesting to talk with.
- You challenge me.

- You have beautiful eyes.

- I really like the way you are around my friends and family.

- I have so much fun with you.

- You have so many qualities I respect.

- I think about you a lot.

- I like the way you make me think about tomorrow.

How precious are these thoughts of you! Wouldn't you trust his proclamation of love if he had already said and meant these other words first? And if he's not saying these sweet things to you and about you, what is he saying? Is he discovering you, appreciating you, encouraging you with what he sees in you? What have you learned about him and about your relationship in six months that indicates to you that there is a potential for further growth and commitment?

Love is such a powerful word, a word we throw around too lightly. This young man may be cautious for good reason, and for your good. He doesn't need to be pressured; he needs to be respected.

There's an old song that contains some vintage truth. Someone once sang it to me, so I'm going to sing it to you, okay? I'll spare you the whole thing. Here it goes:

> Be sure it's true, when you say, 'I love you.' It's a sin—to tell—a lie. Millions of hearts have been broken, just because these words were spoken. I love you. Yes I do. I love you. If you break my heart I will die. So, be sure that it's true when you say 'I love you'. It's a sin—to tell—a lie.
>
> (Mayhew, 1999)

Love,
Laura

Selected Scripture:

Study method:

Truth learned:

Steps I will take to apply it:

My message concerning "Be Sure It's True":

BECOMING TOO DEPENDENT

DEAR LAURA,
How do you know if you are becoming (or if you already are) dependent on your boyfriend or husband?

Reply:

So, how do you determine if you are in fact dependent on your boyfriend or dependent on your husband? Let's start with the boyfriend scenario. Thanks for the opportunity to think through this with you! Here are a few ideas to think about:

- You know you're dependent on your boyfriend when you always have to touch one another when you're together.
- You know you're dependent on your boyfriend when you share an account—email, cell phone, or bank.
- You know you're dependent on your boyfriend when you have no idea what your girlfriends are doing.
- You know you're dependent on your boyfriend when he calls to ask you out, and you cancel any plans you already made just to be with him.

- You know you're dependent on your boyfriend when you have to check with him for what you can do that day, that night, or that weekend.

- You know you're dependent on your boyfriend when you seek his approval or direction over God's.

- You know you're dependent on your boyfriend when you're with him more than you are apart from him.

- You know you're dependent on your boyfriend when he knows your Facebook password.

- You know you're dependent on your boyfriend if you have to ask him for money.

- You know you're dependent on your boyfriend when you have to ask him where you put your keys.

- You know you're dependent on your boyfriend when your friends and/or family tell you that you are.

That last one is where I'll camp. Your Christian girlfriends or the family members with whom you interact daily should be a reliable barometer for whether or not you are becoming dependent on your boyfriend. Ask them—with an open heart and open mind—and see what they think. If you don't have any girlfriends, well, there is another possible indication that you are indeed too dependent on your boyfriend.

Proverbs 27:6 says, "Wounds from a friend can be trusted..." and Proverbs 27:9 reassures us that "Perfume and incense bring joy to the heart, and pleasantness to the friend springs from their heartfelt advice." If you have a Christian girlfriend you are so blessed! Who better to ask about your life than the friend who sees you living it?

"A friend loves at all times..." Proverbs 17:17, so even if you have neglected her, your sweet friend is probably still there for you, watching your life from a distance, and hoping one day you will make time for her again.

Now let's think about marriage for a moment. In a marriage your lives will become so closely intertwined, as God has designed it, that you will absolutely depend on one another. You will be your husband's help mate, and he will be yours. The Proverbs 31 woman was all about meeting the needs of her husband and taking care of the household they shared. However, take note as you read about her, and check her footprints. The vibrant Proverbs 31 gal did not live in her husband's shadow; she made her own—one that reflected the image of God everywhere she went. Read this chapter when you get a chance. The pulse of this woman's heart was her relationship to God

We, together in our marriage, are dependent on God in our individual walk with him, and in the life he has joined us to share. The two become one flesh and there is a physical and emotional dependence that grows in that bond. However, that bond is wrapped up and sealed by his spirit. As we cling to our God for all we are as individuals, and all that we bring to our marriage, our life together is richly blessed.

My husband's provision for me can only go so far, as well as mine for him. And I am so grateful for a husband who directs our decisions not to himself, but to our God, who is our all. Oh sweet girl, for this and for so many other reasons, choose a man who loves God passionately. Who do we really have to depend on in life and in death? "Who have I in heaven but you? And earth has nothing I desire besides you. My flesh and my heart may fail, but God is the strength of my heart and my portion forever" (Psalm 73:25–26).

Thank you for allowing me to think through this with you. How precious is your heart! Please pray about this. Pray about what God wants to teach you, and sweet, sweet heart, please talk to your girlfriend.

Love,
Laura

Selected Scripture:

Study method:

Truth learned:

Steps I will take to apply it:

My message concerning "Becoming Too Dependent":

CAPTIVE HEART, CAPTIVE THOUGHTS

HI, LAURA.

This may sound silly, but I was wondering how I can block out thoughts of a guy when I am at church. I have a relationship with God, I know God lives in my heart and I spend a lot of time worshiping, but sometimes thoughts of this one guy won't leave my head! I know I am going to church for God, and to be further enlightened, but at times I also feel guilty because I know that the guy I have a "crush" on is going to be there and I get excited that I am going to see him. This guy is a believer and spends just as much time at church as I do, so pretty much every time that I am there, he is there too. I feel like at times I have ulterior motives. For example I am definitely getting more "dolled up" for church now-a-days! Is there a need to separate the two? Is this something I should be worried about, or is it just normal? Do you think that God gets angry when the thoughts of the guy are in my head while I am at church? I try very hard to push them out but sometimes those thoughts just won't budge! Thanks for your response!

Reply:

Thank you for writing to me! I totally understand how our thoughts can be a huge battleground. I love that you are concerned about keeping your heart and motives pure. That's awesome! How cool that God speaks to our hearts, ya know? God is guiding you—come on with that! I love that you are looking for a guy in the right place. Keep your eyes open for a guy who shares your love for God! Keep your eyes open for a guy who is passionate about God and will fight for your pure pursuit of God as well! A guy like that is well worth a second thought.

You are right—our thoughts matter to God (Psalm 26:2, Matt. 22:37-38, Phil. 4:8). And the truth of it is, I could try to come up with a ten-step program for keeping your heart, motives, and thoughts on track, but the program would ultimately fail. Jesus knew that, too, which is why he didn't teach that way. He made it so much easier. He taught us in Mark 12:30 that the greatest commandment is "Love the Lord your God with all your heart, and with all your soul, and with all your mind, and with all your strength." He went on to teach, "The second is this: Love your neighbor as yourself." How amazing two commands could cover so much ground in our lives as far as living for God! Be encouraged! Jesus taught us such life-giving truth knowing full well that we could do it with his help, and that this love—God's love—would compel us to live the life we were meant to live in him (see 2 Corinthians 5).

Because we love God, we seek to live for him. In seeking to live for him, we "do" life—or act out our daily lives—differently than we used to. Paul writes in 2 Corinthians 10:5b, "we take captive every thought to make it obedient to Christ." Such strong imagery! And think about that. Paul writes that we take as a prisoner every thought...then what? What does the verse say we do with every thought? We make those thoughts—not free to roam about our heads—but we make them obedient to Christ our Savior—the Savior of even our thoughts!! Again—

strong imagery! We have control over every thought—not vice versa. I love that!

Now, I hear you, my friend, that you're just thinking about this guy. I realize that, and it sounds completely innocent. You're interested in him, of course you'll think about him. We don't want to get all weird by sayin' it's not godly to think about a guy you like. I also understand that you want to look nice for him. So, in the same sense we don't want to say that it's ungodly to want to look pretty. That would just be silly. However, your concern that these thoughts about him and about how you look are influencing your motives is valid. That's where I say, "Uh-huh, absolutely capture those thoughts, each one of them, and make those wandering ideas obedient to Christ."

You're probably thinkin', "Okay that sounds nice, but what does making a thought obedient to Christ look like practically?" Great question! For me, I need God's Word. When I have a self-driven thought in my head, I examine it or compare it with the truth that I have I learned from the Bible. What does God's Word have to say about what I keep considering, what I want to do, and why I want to act a certain way? What is God teaching me about himself or my relationship to him in light of what I keep thinking about? God is faithful to provide the truth I need to capture those thoughts and redirect them. We only know what is good and right to think about, and what is not good and right to think about, or even how to think about the good and the bad, because we go to God in his Word and study with him every day.

Check this out:

> How can those who are young keep their way pure? By living according to your word. I seek you with all my heart; do not let me stray from your commands. I have hidden your word in my heart that I might not sin against you. Praise be to you, Lord; teach me your decrees. With my lips I recount all the laws that come from your mouth. I rejoice in following your statues as one rejoices in great

riches. I meditate on your precepts and consider your ways. I delight in your decrees; I will not neglect your word.

Psalm 119:9-16

God's spirit indwells every believer. He directs us by his Word and his spirit (see Psalm 119:105, John 16:13). Paul wrote in Galatians 2:20 that it is "no longer I who lives, but Christ in me." Amazing! Employ that truth in your life. It's hard to live for Christ with strong intention, but it's worth it.

Consuming thoughts about this guy—or any guy—could lead you into some pretty sad situations. What you think about will motivate your actions. Consuming thoughts about God can only lead to a greater relationship with him, and with others. Ask God to help you consider him above everything and everyone else. He's a good daddy. He knows how to give good gifts—good gifts we need. Ask him to help you capture thoughts and make each one obedient to Christ and to teach you what that looks like for you as his daughter. God knows there is no other relationship that will ever satisfy you like the one he longs for you to have with him. He knows no thought will ever bring greater joy and help to you than those thoughts made obedient to Christ. Embrace every opportunity to learn from God and love him in word, thought, and deed! I sooooo want to encourage you to dive into your Bible and study it to know the heart of the God who loves you passionately! And you'll find yourself thinking about him more, and more, and more, and more, and more, and more... need I say more?

His divine power has given us everything we need for a godly life through our knowledge of him who called us by his own glory and goodness. Through these he has given us his very great and precious promises, so that through them you may participate in the divine nature, having escaped the corruption in the world cause by evil desires. For this very reason, make every effort to add to your faith, goodness; and to goodness, self-control; and to self-control, perseverance; and to perseverance, godliness; and to godliness, mutual affection; and to mutual affection, love. For if you possess these qualities in increasing measure, they will keep you from being ineffective and unproductive in your knowledge of our Lord Jesus Christ.

2 Peter 1:3-8

Love,
Laura

Selected Scripture:

Study method:

Truth learned:

Steps I will take to apply it:

My message concerning: "Captive Heart, Captive Thoughts":

CHOSEN AND LOVED

HI LAURA,
I wanted to talk to you about feeling desirable. I know that sounds really odd, but let me explain:

I am a big girl, as in weight. I'm not the standard for beauty in any way or means, and as a result the only guys that have made me think they would be interested in me have been kind of well, creepers. I never really feel completely beautiful because of my size and just all around looks. The Bible says that as a creation of God, I am his image. But I have to wonder, did God mean before weight or after? Did he mean when I look my best or when I look horrible?

Thank you for making yourself open for questions.

Reply:

Hi, Sweet One. Thank you for your question. You are not alone in your query. You are not alone in your feelings. Thank you for trusting me to seek God and for trusting me with your heart. Thank you for being vulnerable to allow others to experience what we are learning together. Please, take time to read on your own the Scripture that I share with you. In God's Word there is much truth. His Word alone is what discerns our hearts. My words fail; God's do not. God's Word is where I want to encourage you to go. Ask God during your time with him in his Word to show you what he—your Abba—your Daddy—wants you to know about how he feels about you. I want to share some verses that are really wonderful to ponder night and day.

First of all, my friend, God loves you and there is no condition on his love. You have it, and you have always had it. His love is huge for you—so much so that he planned you and chose you for himself—and died for you so that you could realize his love and be with him forever. How's that for adoration?!?! My words fall short of explaining it—but his Word will not. It says in Romans 5:8, "But God demonstrates his own love for us in this: while we were still sinners, Christ died for us."

Think about that—Jesus died for us when we could have cared less for him. When we were disgustingly lost in our self-gratification and our self-indulgences, Jesus thought of us and wanted us to know his love anyway. That amazes me. You, creation of God, are loved without condition. And whether you choose to love him or not, he still loves you. "For God so loved the world that he gave his only Son. That whosoever believes in him, will not perish, but have everlasting life" (John 3:16).

You know that one, right? When Jesus was hanging on the cross, what did he say to God? Do you know this verse? He didn't say, "Get me out of here!" He didn't say, "It isn't worth it—they're undeserving, vile, and ugly people." He didn't even say, "What on earth am I doing here?" He most certainly understood full well what he was doing and why he was doing it, and from that understanding he cried, "Father, forgive them for they do not know what they are doing" (Luke 23:34). Amazing to me! Ignorant in our sin—but nonetheless, still sinning, he chose to die for you and me anyway out of amazing love. He chose to plead for our forgiveness, so that you and I could be in relationship with God. Only unconditional love would do that. Only God is capable of such love. If we choose to believe the truth these verses teach us, we can live a different way—in the realization of God's love. Let me try to explain.

Jesus said in John 15:9, "As the Father has loved me, so have I loved you. Now remain in my love." Great, right! But what does that look like? Think about it. God's love for the son is the same as the Son's love for us. And Jesus told us to remain in his love. We can remain in his love? How, right? What's that when he's not here? We're so stuck in the tangible—the immediate— the visual—the audible—the physical kind of love that satisfies immediately—that this truth is a stretch to grasp. Jesus went on to explain—to give us something more to think about in verse John 15:10, "If you keep my commands, you will remain in my love, just as I have kept my Father's commands."

Now if you're like me, you're goin'"eiyieyie, commands?" Geesh, to lock into his love requires rule following??? Hmmmmm. Not so. We have to remember what Jesus said when he was asked which commands are the most important commands to follow. He said:

> Hear, O Israel: The Lord our God, the Lord is one. Love the Lord your God with all your heart and with all your soul, and with all your mind, and with all your strength. The second is this: Love your neighbor as yourself. There is no commandment greater than these."
>
> Mark 12:29-31

Wow! We have it seemingly so easy, but we make it so hard on ourselves. There is no hoop jumping with God. Love him. Love him, and we will remain in his love. Love others and we will remain in his love. To love him—now that is just where I go... wow...loving God Almighty. What does it look like for me to really love the God of the universe??? With everything that I am? What does it look like for me to love others? Really love them? There's the beauty of our personal relationship to him. He is faithful to teach us—sooooo faithful to walk you by hand through the life that he intended for you—with good things for you to do—with specific lessons from his Word for you to embrace the realization that the Creator of the universe is your God. He is not only passionate about you, but is jealous for your love.

Jesus goes on to say in John 15:11 "I have told you this so that my joy may be in you and that your joy may be complete." If you are lacking in joy when we are supposed to be complete in our quest for joy...which Jesus has completely tied to loving God and loving others...where's the disconnect? Are we unhappy feeling unloved because we have not sought out what it means to love our one God?

Jesus said that heart, soul, mind and strength—every aspect of who I am (we are) is to be about loving one God, and in that my joy—your joy—would be complete. The disconnect with us and that truth is not because God does not love us. It's because we have chosen to move away from him and the constant flow of his love. The flow of his love can always be realized when we remain in him, and follow his Word as Jesus did.

Have you ever seen The Bachelor? The other night, my husband and I tuned in. In this episode, one of the bachelorettes was busted for "entering into a 'relationship' with one of the employees of the show." Yuk! Because she chose some cheap thrill with a staffer dude, she was asked to leave. She chose to have a "relationship" with someone other than "the guy" she was there to fall in love with! And she was sent home not only in shame for her poor choice, but without love that possibly could have been hers for the rest of her life. What do you think? Worth it? Now this is a limited example for sure, but God is your King. We are created to be his. To reflect his glory! He loves us! How gracious he is to show us in our dissatisfaction, in our ache for love, in our ache to feel beautiful. We feel that way because we have chosen someone—something—even doubt—over him.

God's love for you and me does not move. It's our disbelief, our sin, our lack of trust that moves us away from him. He remains in love.

Hear this: you are loved by God. You still with me? You are beautiful to God. Psalm 45:10-11 says, "Listen daughter, and pay careful attention: forget your people and your father's house. Let the king be enthralled by your beauty; honor him, for he is your Lord." Did you catch that? That is for you! Yes, sweet one, you!!! For all of us women who ache in our heart to know that we are beautiful, "Let the king be enthralled by your beauty." How can we let him? We come before him. Wow. Think about that. Going before God. Think about how you might do that.

In the book of Esther, chapter 1, Queen Vashti was asked to come before King Xerxes to honor him with her presence for she was beautiful to look at. He wanted to show her off before the people and nobles of his kingdom. The queen told her attendants to tell the king she would not honor his request. Can you imagine? I mean think about it. Here was this absolutely beautiful woman, a true beauty queen, refusing to let the king admire her. What in the world, right? Why? She was adored by him. He wanted to show her off. Why wouldn't she let him? Why indeed. She was beautiful in his sight! Queen Vashti's choice to refuse the king cost her the throne.

Our King of Kings, enthralled by our beauty, wants us to come before him. And because of Christ, we have entrance into his throne room. What it means to come before him is simple. Know you are loved by him, and boldly seek him, sweet one. We are always in his presence (see Psalm 139). Always. Seek him, and you will find him. Go to him—he is there. Honor him with his request that you would remain in his presence (remember John 15?). That means we make the choice. We are not told why Vashti chose not to go before the king. But, I can think of a thousand reasons rooted in shame and pride why I have refused to go to God. He loves us no matter what we've done. I know that when I do eventually return to him, I regret my unfaithfulness. I feel ugly because of my sin, and I hate that feeling! But then—oh the grace of God! In his presence I am so much more aware of his love! In his presence, he covers me with his love and reminds me that he has forgiven me. I hear in my heart, "Remain in my love."

What does it mean for you to remain in his love? What does it mean to run to nothing, no one, or nowhere else in your quest for love but to God? Use God's Word to help you answer that question. Read the book of John. Ask God to teach you what it means to realize his love—to love him heart, soul, mind and strength. He wants you to know how much you are treasured and how very beautiful you are—and his Word is his love letter to you.

There's a book I'd like to recommend along with the Scripture of course that I've shared with you. *Do You Think I'm Beautiful?* by Angela Thomas is a book that will encourage you and draw you closer to the God who finds you astounding! I'd like to share with you a short passage from it and with that I'll end this letter.

> Being desperate for God keeps us wrapped in his arms at the dance. Being desperate for God has meant for me that I am learning to eat, sleep, drink, and breathe Jesus, climbing over anything that keeps me from him. I realize that it sounds extreme. It sounds like nothing else I've ever done in my life. But I don't know of any other way. To eat, sleep, drink, and breathe Jesus means that I am learning to give priority to the pursuit. It does not mean that I am super spiritual or anywhere close to the arriving. It just means that I am dragging myself into his presence and staying there. It means that I am choosing not to run away from God even in the shame of my sin. I am crying into his shoulder instead of numbing the pain of my life. I have stopped looking everywhere else to be filled and realize that he is the only One who is able. I am putting his Word into my mind even when I am empty or useless or mad.
>
> Desperation is the state of the heart that comes to pursue God for its very life. The spiritual disciplines are the means by which we keep putting ourselves into the presence of God. It means that you keep coming back to prayer even when you cannot see one answer. Keep read-

ing the words in the Bible until the Holy Spirit shows up and gives you understanding. Keep hanging around other believers even when they have disappointed and caused pain. Keep bringing every ugly thought back into captivity. Keep repenting even if you're tired of repenting. Keep singing the praise of worship even when your heart seems to be dying.

What does God do with a desperate woman? I imagine that he smiles as he lifts her up into his presence. Zephaniah said, 'The Lord your God is with you; he is mighty to save. He will take great delight in you, he will quiet you with his love, he will rejoice over you with singing.' Zephaniah. 3:17

(Thomas, 2003)

Thank you for writing to me. I'm excited for the time you have ahead of you in the presence of the King of Kings!!! Ask him to show you how beautiful you are, and to define for you in your skin what it means to live that out.

Love to you beautiful one! Much love!
Laura

Selected Scripture:

Study method:

Truth learned:

Steps I will take to apply it:

My message concerning "Chosen and Loved":

DEAD TO SIN, ALIVE IN CHRIST

DEAR LAURA,
I think, because of my past with several men, and being involved with them sexually, I find myself not wanting to commit to just one man. I get anxious. The lie in my head is, "Hey that guy would be fun; I just want to go on one date with him. I wish I could flirt with him. I need a new guy every week." I hate it! Help! I know I have to fill my mind with Christ's truth and get the lies out, but it's so hard. We all will be punished or have consequences with our sin here on earth, right? Could this be mine? I don't want to struggle with this forever, going into a marriage with these desires would not be good. I'm afraid these lies in my head will never go away.

Reply:
Sheweeee, Girl! Where do I start with your sweet heart? First of all, I need to give you a hug, squeeze you tight, and remind you that you are a daughter of the King of Kings! You are the magnificent, intentional, creation of God Almighty! He chose you before the foundations of the world (Ephesians 1:4)! Yes, you! He created you with a purpose, and he created you to bring him honor, glory, and has equipped you with the ability to do that with all of the riches in Christ Jesus (see Philippians 4:19)! Girl,

you have got it goin' on as far as kingdom success here on earth. You can do all things through Christ, and sin—it has no hold on you, no hold on you in your death, and no hold on you as you live each day here on earth. Christ has conquered your sin nature, and so the old you has died and the new you is alive in Christ—in his eternal, holy, obedient, God seeking, God pleasing nature. Come on with that!!! That is you!!!! And the amazing adventure of discovering exactly what that means—what that looks like, feels like, walks like, talks like, smells like, and tastes like—that's yours for all eternity! Exhaling with you, and taking a deep breath. Did you catch all that? There's more; more that our hearts cannot even fully grasp or contain. We will most assuredly overflow with what we have been blessed to realize and live in Christ Jesus. But will we be open to receive such goodness? Will you?

Thank you so much for your question. I'm going to walk through it with you, okay? You said you think your past with several men makes you unable to commit to one. Not true. You are able. Your past is your past. Can I tell you something really horrible about myself? Okay, here's the ugly truth. Kemper, my sweet husband, is the only—the one and only guy that I committed to—and did not cheat on! Yes!! How awful is that!?!?! Yeah, pretty foul as far as where my sick heart once was—but so, so amazing as to God's hand on this girl's life.

I did not think I was able to commit to one man either. Thank God I chose to believe truth and not the lie I was living! I live for truth now. I believe that God is, and that he rewards those who diligently seek him (see Hebrews 11:6). And you know what? You don't have to be anxious about it. You pray about it. You live one day in that truth. Then you live the next day. Don't think about tomorrow. Live in truth given for today. We live in today, and as today's challenges come, we tackle them as God has prepared us for today. You're prepared for it. That includes sin issues, the need to feel love issues, and the need to be desired issues—all issues. It's all taken care of in Christ. How cool is it to consider that we as believers are slaves to Christ, and he is a loving master that wraps us up in freedom—freedom the heart can only ever know in submission to him. How crazy is that? Yeah, I know! Crazy, and wild, and the ride of a lifetime! It's so good to be God's!

Your issue with commitment is really not so much a part of your past sin, as it is a part of your flesh. We all have a sinful nature—a bent toward sin. I am born with that bent and it is only Christ who can adjust it daily. Here's the difference between you before Christ and you now: you have his spirit within you! He wasn't there before; now he is. The flesh you had is still wrapped around your soul, but your soul is now empowered with the Spirit of the living God. You can't help but want to live for him. If you didn't want to live for him, you wouldn't say, "I hate it" about this struggle! That's the Holy Spirit in you striving to make you in your flesh holy! That's not you, doll; that's God in you! You don't make that holiness want to happen. God in you does that work. The book of Romans is a great place to go and study how this all happens. Check it out! Study it! Don't just read it; study it. Here's a thought to whet your appetite: "For we know that our old self was crucified with him, so that the body ruled by sin might be done away with, that we should no longer be slaves to sin—because anyone who has died has been set free from sin" (Romans 6:6-7).

Diligently, actively applying this knowledge of our Savior is key to living an empowered life. The Word of God is the power pack that enables the flesh to live in the Spirit. That's a big idea, huh?

Look at it this way. Christ—his life—is to be our model. Jesus grew in wisdom and stature with God and man (Luke 2:52). He studied God's Word, and it was God's Word that secured his identity. Jesus was fully God, but we tend to forget that he was fully man, and able to be tempted just as we are able to be tempted. How did he deal with temptation? The Word of God! The Word of God secured his identity, and his purpose, and strengthened him in battle against the enemy. Jesus applied the Word of God to temptation, and he overcame it. It is the same for us. The Word of God secures our identity (2 Corinthians 5:17). The Word of God secures our purpose (John 15:16) and the Word of God will strengthen us in our battle against the enemy (1 John 5:18) who desires to destroy your identity in Christ.

You may say, "Yes, but I have sinned." Yep. You and I both. Just like Eve, we bit the apple. And then you may say, "So, now I know what that forbidden fruit tastes like, and now I am stuck longing after it." Yes, you do know what that fruit tastes like. I'm right there with you. But do you really think that you and I would not have longed for forbidden fruit if we had never tasted it? THAT is our personal "bent" toward sin. Everybody has one. You and I would still have had a sin battle. The difference now is in the way we choose to live after realizing that we made a choice apart from God. We tasted that fruit—and found it lacking. Sin doesn't satisfy. And I know, yes—I definitely know—the device of Satan to make you want to taste it again. Sheweeee that's a mighty pull! But, greater is he that is in you and me, than he that is in the world! (1 John 4:4). You and I can beat the enemy. Out loud—just like Jesus did, we can tell that rattlesnake the truth! So he knows—that we know—that God's Word has all the victory, and Satan's lure cannot entice us to leave the God we love!

Satan's ways have never satisfied me they've only ever brought me sorrow. When I am tempted, I worship God out loud! I tell God, I am tempted to:_____ and I say that ugly sin out loud so I hear the ugliness of it. And out loud I acknowledge that Satan has no secret power to persuade me that the pleasures of sin will ever satisfy me again.

I also make sure that I have loving accountability in my life (James 5:16). It is so good, so loving, and humbling, and just plain (can I say it again?) good, to be able to look someone I respect and love—right in the eye—and admit my temptation to them, and ask for prayer and encouragement. I will never allow an ugly pride streak make me think I don't need to tell a trustworthy friend that I am struggling with temptation. We, my friend, are never beyond being tempted. We are, however, beyond being slaves to sin because of the power of Christ in us. God in his mercy always provides a way out when we are tempted, and that cell phone in your purse can be a lifeline to a godly friend to help you plan and move in the escape. Yeah, that's hard. Living by faith is hard, strong, mighty living. Tell yourself this: "I am able because the Spirit of the living God indwells me." Victorious living happens!

Do not be afraid about what you might never be, sweet girl. Your will is surrendered to God now; he has made you able and he will continue to make you able. God is faithful to complete his beautiful work in you.

"May God himself, the God of peace, sanctify you through and through. May your whole spirit, soul and body be kept blameless at the coming of our Lord Jesus Christ. The one who calls you is faithful, and he will do it" (1 Thessalonians 5:23–24).

Love!
Laura

Selected Scripture:

Study method:

Truth learned:

Steps I will take to apply it:

My message concerning "Dead to Sin, Alive in Christ":

DOES HE BELIEVE?

DEAR LAURA,

I am currently in a relationship and don't know what to do. I met the Lord a year ago and have been walking strong in faith ever since. Although, the more I learn about relationships the more confused I get. My boyfriend believes in Jesus, but he does not have a personal relationship with him or read God's Word. My concern is: do I continue to nurture the relationship in hopes that he'll change? Or do I turn away and walk with someone who is a Christian living out his faith?

Reply:

Thank you for your question. I wish I could speak eye to eye with you on this one. I would love for you to see in my face the love and concern I have for your heart—your life—your future. I am so excited for you, that you have chosen to embrace Christ and live for him. That's awesome! Truly awesome! I want to encourage you to read your Bible—daily. Your new journey with Christ is dependent on God's lessons and his encouragement that he has written for you in his book. Like a baby is dependent on milk to live and grow, you've gotta have God's Word (1 Peter 2:2).

Studying God's Word is a sure way to learn truth and be able to discern what is right for your personal relationship with Jesus.

I want you to know that I am so glad you sent me this question. I have been praying about this reply and praying for you! Many, many girls have asked this very same question. You are not alone.

I am going to turn to the wisdom of Jackie Kendall, who authored *Lady in Waiting*, and I am going to share some verses with you from the Bible. But first I want to go back to your question and what you said specifically, okay?

You said, "My boyfriend believes in Jesus, but he does not have a personal relationship with him or read God's Word." I am taking your words exactly. Those words, sweet heart, speak profound truth—and that truth is your pivot point. I want to share a verse with you:

James 2:18-19 "But someone will say, 'You have faith, I have deeds.' Show me your faith without deeds and I will show you my faith by what I do. You believe that there is one God. Good! Even the demons believe that—and shudder."

Did you catch that? The demons believe in God, and the thought of him freaks them out. They tremble at the thought of God. For example, In Matthew 8:27 when Jesus calmed a storm Jesus' own disciples are asking one another, "What kind of man is this?" They weren't sure who he was, but they followed him. And then a few verses later a demon named Legion clearly identified Jesus as the Son of God, and begged Jesus for mercy (Matthew 8:28-30). Look who is teaching truth! But note this—the cry for God's mercy did not signify allegiance. The demon knew Jesus, and acknowledged the power of Christ over him, but was not willfully obedient to the Son of God.

The verses that follow James 2:18-19 remind us of Abraham's actions because Abraham believed in God, and demonstrated his belief by submission to God. He was willing to sacrifice his only son—the son he was promised, the son he'd been hoping and waiting for all his life! Abraham was ready and willing to do what God asked of him, because he believed in God! Ultimately, Abraham didn't have to kill Isaac. God provided a ram for the sacrifice, but Abraham was willing to, ready to—literally! Isaac was tied to the altar and Abraham held the knife over him ready. Why? Because Abraham's faith was not just a head belief, but active life change—active submission to God—based on what he believed about God. God told Abraham that his act of faith had made him righteous. This is such great truth for you and I to grasp! Check out Genesis 22.

So, let's go back to your insightful description of the young man in your life. He believes, but he has no relationship with Christ. Do you realize what you are saying? He has head knowledge that has made no impact on his heart or his life in any way.

What does this mean for you? God's Word tells those of us who love him, "Do not be yoked together with unbelievers. For what do righteousness and wickedness have in common?" (2 Corinthians 6:14).

Now, this verse specifically says "unbelievers", and you say your boyfriend believes—but belief as defined by James 2 is different from simple—base—head knowledge. Your belief has changed you, hasn't it? Because you believe in Jesus, you are embracing Christ—changing your life to follow him. A lot of people believe that Jesus existed, but that head knowledge has not penetrated their heart and changed them from the inside out. Does that make sense? Because you believe in Jesus, you live for Jesus.

Now, let's go back to 2 Corinthians. What does that verse say? What does God want us to understand about being yoked—or closely connected to—unbelievers, as oxen who pull together in a harness? The Word of God says don't do it! Why? Great question! One that 2 Corinthians answers. Check this out:

> What do righteousness and wickedness have in common? Or what fellowship can light have with darkness? What harmony is there between Christ and Belial (Satan)? Or

65

what does a believer have in common with an unbeliever? What agreement is there between the temple of God and idols? For we are the temple of the living God. As God has said: 'I will live with them and walk among them, and I will be their God, and they will be my people. Therefore, come out from them and be separate,' says the Lord.

2 Corinthians 6:14b–17a

You have nothing, nothing,—N-O-T-H-I-N-G—in common with an unbeliever. You are completely juxtaposed as far as your God sees it. You will live differently in every way, shape, and form; as differently as Jesus and Satan. Because God said so, you should not be with an unbeliever. These words in black and white may be glaring and harsh, and possibly the truth of this message stings your heart. I am sorry for your pain, and I don't mean to offend you, but I know far too well that the harshness of this warning cannot compare to the consequences that will come from ignoring it.

I have been there and done that. I dated someone who "believed" in Jesus, but did not live for Jesus. I loved that man as much as I understood love. I would not break up with him, because I loved him. I married him, and I cried every day of that marriage until it ended in divorce one year later. As painful as breaking up may be, it cannot even begin to compare to the pain of divorce. Do not prolong this relationship in hopes of winning him over to God. End it quickly. As I look back at my refusal to break up with my boyfriend, I have to consider did I truly believe in Jesus? I lived no differently than the man I aligned my heart with. If I did believe, wouldn't I have chosen to do his Word? Hard question, isn't it? If we believe in God, we trust his Word is true, and we do it—no matter what.

God will bless you big time for your belief—for your act of obedience! His promises are sure! "And without faith it is impossible to please God, because anyone who comes to him must believe that he is and that he rewards those who earnestly seek him." Hebrews 11:6

Please allow me to introduce you to Jackie Kendall, author and speaker. In her book, *Lady in Waiting*, she shares powerful truth for you and me to consider together, because God is a good daddy who longs to protect us.

> Here comes the bride all dressed in … chains! 'Hey wasn't that supposed to be "all dressed in white"'? The last word in the chorus was changed to 'chains' because she made the unwise choice of marrying an unbeliever. The chains symbolize what she has to look forward to as a believer married to an unbeliever. The Word of God speaks clearly about a partnership with an unbeliever. When a single woman experiences a prolonged period of datelessness, loneliness tempts her to compromise her conviction concerning dating a growing Christian. Her dateless state may pressure her to surrender to the temptation of dating an unbeliever. She may justify such a date in the guise of being a witness for Jesus. Many single women have been trapped emotionally with an unbeliever when it all began with 'missionary dating'. Ponder this: every unbelieving marriage partner arrived as an unbeliever on the first date. As trite as it may seem, every date is a potential mate. Avoid dating an unbeliever.
>
> (Kendall et al, 1995)

Do you love God? Do you? Love him then, with all your heart, soul, mind, and strength. Do not cling to this relationship like it is your all and all. It isn't. God is your all in all. This decision is pivotal for you, sweet girl. Hugely pivotal! Move in your faith. Turn to God. Embrace and serve him. You will find yourself in the midst of great love. "Those who cling to worthless idols forfeit God's love for them. But I, with shouts of grateful praise will sacrifice to you. What I have vowed I will make good. I will say, 'Salvation comes from the Lord'" (Jonah 2:8–9).

I am praying for you. Please know that!
And remember—believers do!

Love!
Laura

Selected Scripture:

Study method:

Truth learned:

Steps I will take to apply it:

My message concerning "Does He Believe?":

FACELESS, NAMELESS, SERVANT

DEAR LAURA,

How as women should we witness to guys without them thinking we are interested in them? Is there a difference in the way a girl should witness to another guy when she is dating someone?

Reply:

Hey! Thanks for your question! So pumped to hear that sharing the Gospel is on your heart! Jerry Gillis, the Senior Pastor at The Chapel at CrossPoint in Buffalo, NY was actually introduced to Christ by a young lady named Kay when he was nineteen years old. Her passion was Jesus, and Jesus directed her in his mission to reach out to Jerry with the good news of Jesus Christ. God uses women in his purpose to propel the Gospel.

When we walk closely with our God, we hear his direction (see John 10). His Word is the lamp to our feet, so we can see and examine each step we take; his Word is the light to our path, so we see can see where we are headed (see Psalm 119). When we walk closely with our God, he grows us in his wisdom and his knowledge (see Colossians 2). When we walk closely with our God, we open our hearts wide—every door—and ask him to know us, test us, try us, and show us what is offensive to him, and lead us in a new way—the way that is everlasting (see Psalm 139). When we walk closely with our God we guard our heart with him—his Word—because everything we do then flows from a pure source (see Proverbs 4:20-23). When we walk closely with our God, we pray what he wants us to pray; we go where he wants us to go; we love who he wants us to love, and how he wants us to love (see 1 Thessalonians).

Walk closely with God. Let him lead you. You are the servant of God. How amazing!!!! Your direction comes from him. Is that just crazy goodness or what?! If God blesses you with the urgency to invite someone, guy or gal, to attend an event, Bible study, or service at your church, move in that obediently. If God blesses you with the opportunity to share with someone—guy or gal—the story of how you came to know Christ, move in that obediently. If God blesses you with the opportunity to share the good news of Christ with someone—guy or gal—move in that obediently. The beauty of every opportunity is that you are God's chosen instrument, his chosen vessel for the purpose of reaching out to that one person in that moment in just that way. Focus on God. Then you will be confident with pure intentions, pure direction, pure thoughts, and pure results.

In the small groups at Vintage, the young adult ministry where we serve, guys are with guys and girls are with girls. Guys and girls are different in their struggles, in their needs, in their experiences, and even in the way they communicate with one another. So if you realize that a guy that you have shared Christ with is relying on you for help in the area of spiritual growth, direct him to godly men who will be able to meet him where he's at and relate to him with the Word of God and what it means to be a man seeking God fully.

I am excited for you as you seek God for his purposes in your passion to proclaim him to everyone! Grateful for you! Praying for you!

> I took you from the ends of the earth; from its farthest corners I called you. I said, 'You are my servant'; I have chosen you and have not rejected you. So do not fear, for I am with you; do not be dismayed, for I am your God. I will strengthen you and help you; I will uphold you with my righteous right hand.
>
> Isaiah 41:9-10

Servant; faceless—nameless—God's.

Love!
Laura

Selected Scripture:

Study method:

Truth learned:

Steps I will take to apply it:

My message concerning "Faceless, Nameless, Servant":

FAITH MOVES

DEAR LAURA,
What if you are currently living with your boyfriend, sharing an apartment, a lease agreement, and planning to get married? I'm kind of stuck.

Reply:

Who told you that you're stuck? Is that you talkin' to yourself? Because you are wrong about that. You are as free as the fresh air on the other side of your door. Your prison is your own thoughts, sweet girl.

Yes, I understand that the situation is knee deep in details—details that are tied to your heart not just to stuff you move in boxes. Sweetheart, you have a wonderful, full-life choice to make that is your freedom. Turn your life around. Do a 180. What a miracle when God changes our mind! It is so exciting to know that our God is pressing his truth onto your heart. You know that is him, don't you?

Yes, life change takes serious determination, work, discipline, but first and foremost comes heart change. Life change that follows heart change is of God. He's working on your heart! He's got all the strength you need! Believe it! How desperately God wants you to experience life in him, to walk in his way, his love, his faithfulness, and to abide in him. We can't abide in him and live in sin.

We always have a choice which is the goodness of our God to give us one. We always have the ability which is the goodness of our God to give us his spirit. Would he give you direction, without making you able? Absolutely not! I want to encourage you to choose him—fully—which means moving out from the apartment you share with your boyfriend. Today. Yes. Today. Don't sleep there another night. You know what you need to do; now do it. Watch how God will move on your behalf when you give him lordship over your life! Girl! Watching God work!!! How incredible is that? And what a testimony of his goodness you'll be singing!!!

I could go on and on about God's faithfulness to those who chose him based on blind faith. Read Hebrews chapter 11. Nobody saw God—they simply believed. Rahab is my favorite, because, well…she was a harlot, and she simply heard of the God of Israel and how he had parted the Red Sea, and was coming to the city of Jericho to defeat it on behalf of his people, Israel. She only heard of God. She hadn't even seen his miracles. Rahab only heard of what God had done and she wanted in with Israel's God. God's power drew her to him, and his power helped her break free from her old life. God took her from what could have been her death into a new life with him and with his people. She left behind everything she ever knew to become a woman of God. And God included her in his eternal story of faith that pleased him (Hebrews 11). You think her silk, perfume, and boyfriends could ever measure up to that kind of blessing? Rhetorical question of course, but can you imagine the life change that was ahead of this woman once she chose God? Once she renounced her lifestyle, do you think embracing what it meant to follow after a God she could not see was easy?

I would think her life of faith was full of still more challenges; challenges like living among judgmental Israelite women, and challenges of trying to learn a whole new way of eating, drinking, loving others, and even worshipping the God she had chosen. Obviously Rahab endured as an Israelite, and only God knows how very much, but we can read how great her eternal blessing in Matthew 1. Her name is listed among those who are the physical ancestor of our Savior.

What if Rahab had chosen to stay with her people in Jericho—the life that was easy, known, and precious to her as she could define precious from her limited point of view? What if you choose to stay right where you are? Or, what if you didn't? What if you with bold faith, like Rahab, choose God?

Have you heard of Jonah and the whale? Jonah, having disobeyed God was stuck in the belly of a great fish. What a predicament to be in, huh? How would you get out of that one? Not much packing to do, but a lot of praying. Jonah prayed in chapter 2 verses 8-9, "Those who cling to worthless idols forfeit God's love for them. But I, with shouts of grateful praise will sacrifice to you." Jonah realized he had made his desires his god. He realized that to experience the love of the one true God is to live for him—which will always be a sacrifice. However, the blessing that comes from that sacrifice invokes shouts of grateful praise.

Sweetness, if I myself had not experienced that truth in my own life, I would not be writing this to you. It's true—and I can't stop talking about it—writing about it. Lord, help my family when I start singing about it! If I want you to know how amazing this life in Christ truly is, can you imagine how much more your heavenly Daddy wants you to know it? He loves you far more than I could ever hope to love you! I hope you hear all my love in my words to you—but even more so in God's words from his book on which I am relying.

I love Psalm 119. Please read it. Read all of it, and ask God to grip your heart with his understanding, his truth. I want to share some of it with you. It says in verses 1-4:

Blessed are those whose ways are blameless, who walk according to the law of the Lord. Blessed are those who keep his statutes and seek him with all their heart—they do no wrong but follow his ways. You have laid down precepts that are to be fully obeyed. Oh that my ways were steadfast in obeying your decrees! Then I would not be put to shame when I consider all your commands. I will praise you with an upright heart as I learn your righteous laws. I will obey your decrees; do not forsake me utterly.

Psalm 119:1-4

Can you hear the writer's heart for God? Such heartfelt understanding of truth! God's loving, faithful truth invokes determination, passion, and movement from sin toward God. How will you ever know, precious girl, how good it is to dwell with God and to walk his ways unless you let go of what you are deceived into believing is so precious—so right for your life—and embrace the one true God? We cannot embrace him, while clinging to our own life—our own way—our sinful choices. He wants all of us. All of our life, our heart, our soul, our mind, and our strength fully devoted (see Mark 12:29-30).

In Matthew 19:16–22, Jesus has a conversation with a man about what it takes to find eternal life. Jesus ultimately tells him, go sell all you have and follow me. When the man heard Jesus' direction, he walked away from Christ very sad, because his wealth—his "stuff" pile—was huge. Why did Jesus' instruction him make the man so sad? Maybe you can answer that question just based on your own circumstances.

It's hard to let go of what we have chased after, held, lived by, thought about, become, and deemed most precious to live a whole new way—a way that requires blind faith. The man Jesus spoke to would have to let go of all he had accumulated, depended on, invested in, worked so hard for to embrace following Christ. He would have to blindly believe that life—eternal life—is in Christ and nothing else. That takes some kinda courage, huh? Whoever is a Christ follower understands that living for Jesus requires courage, and if we don't understand this premise, we must closely examine our "followship", or in other words, the way in which we live for Christ. I would love for you to read *Followship*, by Pastor Jerry Gillis. Allow me to share a brief passage from a chapter entitled Courage:

> If you do not walk by faith, then you really do not need courage. There is a sense of comfort in plotting our own course and controlling our own destiny. You don't need courage for that. But try living by faith and making some decisions that reflect you are living by faith, and then you will lose all sense of comfort and control. You will need courage. In our journey with Jesus, I believe that the virtue of courage is designed for the follower that is willing to take steps of faith.
>
> (Gillis, 2005)

In choosing Christ, we courageously turn from everything in our life that does not honor him (1 Corinthians 5-6). In choosing Christ we make him our leader, our guide every single day (John 14-15). In choosing Christ, we read, study, learn, and think about his Word and regard it as the one source of all truth; not only do we deem it the truth but we acknowledge our desperate need for it (Ephesians 1-4). And we put that truth to work in our lives daily as God, our teacher, helps us to learn it, know it, apply it, and bring him glory as his children following hard after it (Ephesians 5-6). Sheweee, take a breath!

Life in him is sacrifice, my friend. But, Jesus said whoever loses his life for his sake would find it (Matthew 16:25). He provided instruction for what that looks like, and gave us promises for the blessings that would satisfy us beyond what the world has to offer. Please read Psalm 119, and be encouraged and challenged in what God is placing on your heart to do. Girl, yes you are taking a huge leap. Yes, you are letting go and falling back into some unknown, but the faithful, loving arms of our unseen God will not forsake you.

> How loving is your dwelling place, Lord Almighty! My soul yearns, even faints, for the courts of the Lord, my heart and my flesh cry out for the living God. Even the sparrow has found a home, and the swallow a nest for herself, where she may have her young—a place near your altar, Lord Almighty, my King and my God. Blessed are those who dwell in your house; they are ever praising you. Blessed are those whose strength is in you, whose hearts are set on pilgrimage. As they pass through the Valley of Baka (an oasis found on a desert journey to the temple), they make it a place of springs; the autumn rains also cover it with pools. They go from strength to strength till each appears before God in Zion. Hear my prayer, Lord God Almighty; listen to me, God of Jacob. Look on our shield, O God; look with favor on your anointed one. Better is one day in your courts than a thousand elsewhere; I would rather be a doorkeeper in the house of my God than dwell in the tents of the wicked. For the Lord God is a sun and shield; the Lord bestows favor and honor; no good thing does he withhold from those whose walk is blameless. Lord Almighty, blessed are those who trust in you.
>
> Psalm 84

I pray you are encouraged. I pray you are motivated by him. I pray you start packing, and don't look back with doubt. Move forward with your faith—into new life. I hear you. I know what you're asking. How long should you be on your own? Time is nothing for God. He wants your heart. All of it. Stay on your own; don't marry this young man, until your life—until your boyfriend's life—is clearly defined by God. Then you'll have something precious to help you begin your marriage and secure it. Can you even imagine?!? Oh I can see it now! Your wedding, your marriage, your lives together to glorify God—what a celebration that will be!

Come to Vintage at The Chapel at CrossPoint, or if you can't get there go to our website at www.vintagetruth.com, okay? You can watch us live or tune in to see past messages that have been saved on our website for online viewing.

Seek God, grow and learn with people who are seeking God, growing and learning about him together. And if you need help packing, guess what? Ask those same people! Help will be right there! God is faithful!

Turn. Embrace. Serve. Faith moves.

Love!
Laura

Selected Scripture:

Study method:

Truth learned:

Steps I will take to apply it:

My message concerning "Faith Moves":

THE BACK OF MY MIND

DEAR LAURA:
I recently broke up with my boyfriend. We weren't together very long, and for a while I kept thinking in the back of my mind that this relationship wouldn't build me up in Christ. After I broke up with him I felt immense guilt and wished I had never done it. During our relationship I would ask my boyfriend about God, and it felt awkward and somewhat of a topic to avoid. Do you think I should have asked different questions? Did I jump to a conclusion and assume his faith wasn't strong since he wasn't as sharing about it as I was? These questions continue to float through my head, and I want to make sure that I made the absolute right decision. Although it did surprise me that after I broke things off he told me he thought that perhaps that God was letting this happen because he wanted him to get his life together and get closer to him...So I do believe I did make the right decision. I just wish I had confirmation. Thank you very much.

Sincerely,
A hurting young woman.

Reply:

Thank you for writing to me! I hate that you are hurting! I am so sorry! Breaking up stinks, no matter what. You shared your heart with someone, and he shared his with you and now that closeness and time—for whatever reason—is over. You are going to be in a flux of pain and regret for a little while...hopefully very little. Don't let your heart lead you though. You made a hard decision based on truth. And you can always rest in the truth no matter what.

"But when he, the Spirit of truth comes, he will guide you into all the truth" (John 16:13a).

"You make known to me the path of life; you will fill me with joy in your presence, with eternal pleasures at your right hand" (Psalm 16:11).

"See if there is any offensive way in me, and lead me in the way everlasting" (Psalm 139:24).

"Whether you turn to the right or to the left, your ears will hear a voice behind you, saying, 'This is the way, walk in it.'" Isaiah 30:21

The verses that I shared with you are truth. You were being led by God's spirit. Maybe in the moment you could not tie a verse to that direction you felt, but if you seek him in his Word now, you will find the word that will articulate that nudge.

Take some time and consider carefully why you felt that this relationship did not build you up in Christ. Get a glimpse of the actions in your relationship that fueled that Spirit-led realization. There is a verse that God will guide you to know and rest in. Of that I am sure. Our heart is so deceitful, sweet one! Ugh! I wish it were not so. But even that truth—that ugly truth about our heart—is Abba God wisdom for us to grow by and that comes from God's Word in love (see Jer.17:9).

Lovingly our God has made me see and realize that his Word is trustworthy. I deceive myself time and again. And God—our patient Daddy—directs and corrects and instructs us in love.

Even (and this part kills me) when I did not know one verse, God was teaching me his Word—by his spirit—so that later, when I read it, I realized his hand was on my life. God was speaking to me, and now I have the words to the voice I knew I had heard all along. Crazy sweetness! Crazy and miraculous and unbelievably mouthwatering is my time in God's Word, because now I just want to find and hear his voice, so that I hear him and do not miss his words over my own heart.

Hear me out, okay? You have had this directing from God, my friend. He is directing you by his spirit if you have indeed received him and now follow him. And he will be faithful to show you the words for that inner voice—that back of your mind ache—if you seek him in his Word. It will all become so crystal, bright path, clear that your faith will bolster! Truly, truly, truly!

So are you in the Word of God?? Go for it! Seek that Word that he is drawing you to know. Where do you begin? Great question! Begin right where you are. Ask God, "Where would you have me read, and what would you have me know about you—and what would you have me know about how to live for you?" And then, let him guide you.

I want to close with some decision making guidelines that Wes Aarum, the young adult pastor at The Chapel at CrossPoint in Buffalo, New York, outlined to help us walk in wisdom. Here they are:

1. Does it master me? Does it exercise control in my life or influence me in a wrong way? 1 Corinthians 6:12

2. Will it help someone else's walk with God? 1 Corinthians 8:12-13; Matthew 5:16

3. Is it beneficial in any way to me spiritually, mentally, physically? 1 Corinthians 10:23; Mark 12:30

4. Does it bring Glory to God? 1 Corinthians 10:31

5. Does it slow me down spiritually? Hebrews 12:1

6. Does it help me to be a good example of Jesus to non-believers? Colossians 4:5

7. Does it encourage me to be pure and holy? 2 Timothy 2:22

8. Is this the wise choice? Ephesians 5:5-17

Please know I have prayed for you. My prayer is that through all of this you will realize the love of your heavenly Daddy, trusting his spirit within you and seeking always the words that he has written to match that Spirit of truth!

Praying this for you and me! "May my cry come before you, Lord; give me understanding according to your word...May my lips overflow with praise, for you teach me your decrees. May your hand be ready to help me, for I have chosen your precepts" (Psalm 119:170, 172-173).

Love!!!
Laura

Selected Scripture:

Study method:

Truth learned:

Steps I will take to apply it:

My message concerning "The Back of My Mind":

FORGIVE OR FORGET HIM

DEAR LAURA,

This question is probably not one you are used to. If I thought I could find the answer in a relationship book I would have already because I've read like 30 Christian relationship books so this one is not typical. I have lived a pure life for the past 4 years, never had sex and gave that area of my life completely to God 4 years ago when I was 17. I changed from reading romance novels and watching chick flicks to eliminating most movies and reading Christian relationship books instead. I wanted to know God's way and follow it.

Upon God's constant peace and leading I began a relationship with a Christian young man 3 months ago, and recently he confessed that he struggled with pornography from middle school until the end of freshmen year in college (2 years ago). I want so badly to forgive him and move on, but I know for a fact that these images will forever be in his mind and that he is obviously very weak to this temptation. I also know that it plagues my generation 10 fold. I was content with finding my all in the Lord and now I feel tempted to break it off because I'm scared to death to marry someone who is so vulnerable to porn. I don't even want him to ever see me naked knowing the standard I'm up against.

What happens when I've had 3 children and my body is no longer desirable? Do men just not understand how deeply their decision to fill their head with this garbage affects us women? Do they know that it doesn't just hurt them it kills their future wives and makes them feel like nothing more than sex objects? Why is it that even the Christian men are no different? Do any of them live faithfully?

What's even worse is that I have prayed so much for my future husband's purity, especially that year when my boyfriend struggled with it the most. Did God not hear my prayers!? Or should I take this as a sign that my boyfriend is not my future husband even though I have felt God leading me to stay in this relationship? Am I just unforgiving? I am mad. I'm mad that he gave into sin and I am even madder that it has made me question God's faithfulness to answer my prayers. Why didn't he intervene or protect him?

Please, as a Christian woman who married a man who struggled with this, help!

Reply:

Hi, my friend! I am sorry you are frustrated. I want to encourage you to let God's peace rule your heart; the defining word being "let". You have a choice to let God's peace rule your life. Isn't that incredible? Behind curtain number 1: peace. Behind curtain number 2: frustration and anger. Which one will you choose? God's word brings peace. It's not magic. It's truth. What we choose to do with that truth makes all the difference. You with me?

I want to share truth with you that will help you embrace the peace God has waiting for you. Please know I am not the answer to all your concerns. God is. It is on his Word that I rely for this letter to you. And it is to his Word I hope you will turn when you evaluate all I am going to say to you. Please consider his Word most carefully. God's Word cannot fail. I am so excited to hear about your passion for God. That you gave your life to him is precious, powerful, and exciting. There is so much in store for you in Christ! You are a beautiful, multifaceted creation of God. Your relationship to one man for the rest of your life is only one potential aspect of your total being. Don't limit yourself to see only one part of all you are.

You've read a lot of Christian books on relationships. There's so much more to know of God and so much to realize about his purpose for your life! Check out the Proverbs 31 woman. She had much to do about town, and her dealings extended far beyond that of her relationship to her husband. We have so much to learn about God! Move on in your studies, sweet girl! *Peace Making Women* by Tara Klena Barthel and Judy Dabler is a great book. If you like to be intellectually stimulated, any book by Lee Strobel, C.S. Lewis and Erwin McManus are a few authors worth checking out. Kay Arthur has a lot of books that will help unlock God's Word for you. Have you read any of Beth Moore's books? I love her studies. I think you might, too. Read on, my friend!

Now, let's talk about your concerns with your boyfriend. He is a believer in Christ and he has confessed to you his past struggle with pornography. His struggle, although past, is going to continue. You're right. However, his struggle now will look very different than it did then. He is probably walking in victory now—at least I hope he is, but he is still probably battling the attacks of temptation that pornography offers in this day and age. Maybe not every day, and maybe not to a difficult degree—but the struggle is still probably very real at times.

Consider with me your own sin nature. You still sin, right? You probably feel the temptation before you commit the sin, correct? Do you have victory over past sins—like gossip for example? I don't know you personally or if this is or has been an issue in your life, but let's use it for the sake of an easy example. This could have been a constant source of sin in your life once upon a time, and now because you have grown in your relationship with

God, it isn't. You might feel an urge to gossip every now and then, but you work through it with God's Word in your mind and heart. And maybe you have shared this struggle with a friend who prays for you and with you, and may hold you accountable by asking you how you are doing in your walk with God from time to time. Sin is sin. Although the consequences and specifics are different, it's all vomit to God. It all makes him sick. So consider that your sin, like your boyfriend's, can be forgiven and overcome, and can help bring glory to God as he changes you. Does that make sense?

Back to your boyfriend. The temptation to look at pornography can be a very difficult struggle. True, some may struggle with this temptation more than others; not all men are wired the same way. But the fact is that the man in your life—in my life—is wired that way. What are you and I going to do about it? You may choose to walk away from your boyfriend entirely. But you may find yourself in the same situation with another guy all over again.

So, here's my thinking as influenced by God's Word. The man in my life is my husband, so that's slightly different from your situation, but there are some similarities for you to consider. He is flesh and blood. He has a sin nature (it comes with his skin). However, he loves God. He made a defining choice to turn from his sin (from idols) and serve God (1 Thessalonians 1:9). Do you see evidence of life change in your boyfriend? If the men in our lives want to live for God, then their commitment to God is evident. My friend, I see evidence of my husband's love for God all over his life—consistently. I choose to love and forgive, and encourage the man in my life with God's Word and God's love, and I do not hold his past against him in any way, shape, or form. We grow together in Christ, and not apart. His past is triumphed and overshadowed by the Spirit of God that indwells him. This is clear and real to me every single day (2 Corinthians 4). Can you say this of your boyfriend? Your answer to that question is critical to the future of your relationship.

Consider this, sweet one: Jesus never said that we would not be tempted if we followed him. You won't find that anywhere. Look up temptation in the concordance of your Bible and see what you find. You'll be amazed. Jesus himself was tempted in every way we are tempted. Crazy, huh? God facing temptation? The key difference is he did not succumb to it. And in the book of James we read that if we resist the devil—as Jesus did time and again by using the Word of God—the devil will flee from us (James 4:7).

Victory is ours daily with one critical element: choice. As believers we aren't temptation free—we are free to choose Christ. Your boyfriend, sweet one, is going to be tempted. You are still tempted to sin, aren't you? Maybe pornography does not taunt you, but something does. And for both of you—however you are wired in your flesh, you both have a choice. What are you going to do in the midst of that temptation? That he told you he struggled with it is very cool to me. He is laying it out on the table—to be held accountable and to be prayed for in his struggle. I respect that. Trust and accountability are two critical relationship elements. I'm sure you have read that in your studies. Confessing our sins to each other is an amazing gift to help us heal from those sins (James 5:16). He probably doesn't tell everybody about this, but he chose to tell you. What you do with that information is very defining for both of you in your relationship.

Did you hear him out concerning the action he has taken to rid himself of this sin? Has he told a close friend to help keep him accountable? Has he put a block on his computer? Has he put his computer in a place where he is not alone somewhere? Whatever measures he has taken to keep his life free from sin are to be respected.

I do know pornography is readily available and it's a fight for godly men, even pastors, to avoid it. Please pray for godly men in our nation! Please pray for our pastors (2 Chronicles 7:14)! Specific to your boyfriend, you said, "I know those images will be forever in his mind and that he is obviously very weak to this temptation." Sweet one, God is a healer, and in him we are strong. I believe this. I live this truth daily. The images locked in my mind from my own past sin issues could prevail if it were not for God's Word that has washed over me and changed my life and my husband's life. Psalm 119! True we could recall them at any given moment, but because of the love of Christ, together we choose not to. And he—his love—has made all the difference. God forgives, blesses, redeems, restores, washes, heals, and empowers us to live out of purity, grace, and truth.

I could go on and on about the value of God's Word in my life and how it has changed me and my husband. We withstand the temptations that the enemy seeks to destroy us with because of God and our love for him, and second to that our love for one another. Kemper's love for God is what makes him love me beautifully. My love for God is what teaches me to love and honor my husband. I cannot stress this enough. If you are in a relationship with a man who loves God with all of his heart, soul, mind and strength, and you are a woman who loves God with all your heart, soul, mind and strength, then you do not need to fear what will become of a potential marriage. Individually you will grow in Christ—and together you will grow strong in Christ, and your marriage will be blessed.

Forgiveness is hard, but it is worth it. I most certainly do not want you to be ignorant of what could be an ongoing sin in your boyfriend's life. And please hear me...I said sin which is the act and not the temptation. Be sure—if you remain with him—that he has made every effort to protect himself from triggers that might foster this temptation, and that he has some good Christian friends that are living for God with him. You should see evidence of his love for God consistently in his life. Any inconsistencies are worth noting and talking about together. Be wise. Be slow to anger (James 1:19); balance your inquiries with love, patience and grace. In other words, don't disrespect him. But, yes, my friend—if you really love this guy, yes, you need to forgive him. You need to love him authentically and that means offering him complete forgiveness. If you can't forgive him, then love him enough to let him go so that he might have the opportunity to experience this kind of love from someone who can offer it. Because, ultimately, I believe someone will. Will you go to your Bible concordance, look up the word forgive or forgiveness, and take some time with God to study those passages? I think you will be encouraged about what God has to say with regard to forgiving others.

Purity is a beautiful thing to pray for concerning your future spouse. I want to encourage you, that God has heard your prayers and has your future mate protected completely. He died for his sins past, present, and future—just as he died for yours. Your boyfriend made a choice that has hurt you, and for that he is seeking your forgiveness. But please consider this—his sin is against God and dear one, you are not above God who forgave him already even in the midst of his sin. Continue to pray for him—that he will live a life worthy of the Lord (Colossians 1:9-11). Prayer is powerful. Our God is faithful, and able, and he will accomplish his good and perfect will.

Love!!!
Laura

Selected Scripture:

Study method:

Truth learned:

Steps I will take to apply it:

My message concerning: "Forgive or Forget Him":

FREEDOM FROM GUILT

DEAR LAURA,
Is masturbation wrong? I know that I know that it is far more common among men, and I even believe that it is ok for men to masturbate as long as they do not accompany the action with lustful thoughts, but I feel like men have more of an excuse because there can be a physical need for that "release" where there is no comparable need for women.

I feel so dirty, scummy and low because I've stumbled onto masturbation. It all began by accident and I didn't even know what it was that I was doing, but that doesn't really matter because now I completely understand what I'm doing. I feel gross because I think of this as something a man can do because men have a high sex drive, and I think it makes me feel like this perverted sex addict in a way, even though I haven't had sex. I don't know, I can't really explain how I feel without sounding like a five year old who doesn't know the words to describe how she's feeling.

I've tried to stop, I've memorized verses for when I feel tempted, and I've been praying, but I haven't been really successful yet. I think that the way it makes me feel is proof that it's wrong, but am I guilting myself excessively? It's not like I accompany my action with lustful thoughts or porn or anything, it's just a physical gratification. Is this wrong?

I'm currently in a relationship and we plan to get married after we graduate from college. I've discussed this with my boyfriend to some extent but I feel awkward doing so. I know he masturbates, but I don't think any less of him. I just don't know that I can be allowed the same justification. His opinion was that because we can't have sex for 2 more years, it may not be a bad thing to satisfy it somehow without allowing lustful or sexual thoughts to accompany it. I don't know. Partly I feel like it could be ok if I don't make an addiction out of it; for example, if I am not doing it every day or depending on it or unable to resist it, but maybe if I do it occasionally it could be ok. Like eating ice cream—you can enjoy it occasionally but if you overindulge you will become a glutton, which is both unhealthy and sinful and accompanied by a lack of self-control. On the other hand, I think that it could possibly increase my sexual desire and make the struggle for purity with my boyfriend even more of a challenge. Or, it could cause me to be more prone to thinking lustful sexual thoughts, which is something I want to avoid and stay away from all together. Or finally, it could really be a sin and I just haven't fully acknowledged that yet, and every time I do it I push myself farther away from God—and that I definitely don't want. I mean, is this part of sexual immorality that the Bible speaks so highly against?

What should I do? Do you have any answers or advice for me, Laura? Are there any books or anything I can read to help me figure out on my own what is appropriate for me according to God?

Please send me any advice you can give. Thanks.

Reply:

"I will walk about in freedom for I have sought out your precepts" (Psalm 119:45).

Thank you for writing to me. Thank you for trusting me with your heart. Please know I do not take lightly that I get the opportunity to share God's Word with you and that I personally get to encourage you to love and seek our heavenly Father. What a gift to my life!

I am not sure how long you have been a follower of Jesus Christ, but what I do know is that you are presently. When we choose to live for God you know he promised to put his spirit within us (see 1 Corinthians 6:19)—to give us his help and his strength in this life for his purposes. However, we are learning and growing in this gift and for that I want to encourage you (and myself) that God is a good, faithful, patient, loving teacher. It is our goal as believers—daily—to walk by the Spirit because in doing so we reflect Jesus Christ who died that we might live a full life that is only possible—only desirable—by his spirit.

> So I say, walk by the Spirit, and you will not gratify the desires of the sinful nature. For the sinful nature desires what is contrary to the Spirit; and the Spirit what is contrary to the sinful nature. They are in conflict with each other, so that you are not to do whatever you want.
>
> Galatians 5:16-17

This is for all of us, my friend: men and women. Will you think carefully with me about how this truth presses in on the question you have asked?

My sweet friend, I can teach you the do's and don'ts of the law of God. God has all of the laws clearly identified for us in his Word, so that they are easily understood by even those who do not know him. God gave us the law to teach us guiding principles for life, and it is good to know his laws as they reflect the character of a holy God. They reflect God's love for his people. They are full of blessing, provision and protection. And the laws remind us how desperate all people are for a savior. How merciful for God to rescue us from our own self-destruction. Our God fulfilled the requirement of the law in his Son—the law giver and keeper—and then our merciful God gave us his spirit so that instruction, wisdom, protection, blessing, provision, and the presence of our God would be ours for always.

I will give them an undivided heart and put a new spirit in them; I will remove from their heart of stone and give them a heart of flesh. Then they will follow my decrees and be careful to keep my laws. They will be my people, and I will be their God.

Ezekiel 11:19-20

Our faithful God has done this, and it is evidenced in you by your letter. He is speaking to you, my friend. I can take you verse by verse about sexual immorality, but my concern is what will you choose to hear? God is clearly speaking to you. So when you go to his Word with me, will you hear God's love for you and how unselfish he is in his love? Will you hear his desire for you to walk in freedom from guilt? Will you hear that he longs for you to be filled with his love, full, overflowing, and completely satisfied? Will you hear that Jesus wants you to walk in the same loving relationship he had with God and others? Will you hear that Jesus never sought to gratify himself in any way, because he didn't have to? He was satisfied.

God's Word is consistent. He desires for his people to be holy as he is holy. His law does not make us holy; his law reflects his presence in his people. The blessing of God over his chosen people was his laws that enable them to abide with him and be satisfied by him. We who are called by his name get to reflect his perfect love to a world that loves selfishly. If we examine any of the laws of God, we can clearly see self-gratification is opposed to the Spirit of God. Sex within the context of marriage is not opposed to God, even pleasure is not opposed to God. He gave us food for the body, and sex for marriage, and beauty to behold. God is not opposed to pleasure. He is opposed to selfish motives. Sex, in all its amazing facets, dear heart, is for marriage, where husband and wife seek to love one another, not alone—but together.

What is beautifully evidenced in you is the Spirit of God calling you to hear him. Let me encourage you to get alone with God—with his Word—and ask him to teach you by his Word.

Not your voice. Not your boyfriend's voice. But his written Word, verse by life-changing verse what he would have you know and realize about his love, provision and blessing over your life—that is his Word.

The entire book of Galatians is Paul's letter to a people who needed clarification about what it meant to be under the law of Judaism—and what it meant to be free in Christ. Paul writes in chapter 3 that before we came to faith we were held in custody of the law—locked up. It was the law—the do's and don'ts that controlled us until Christ came so that we might be justified—set free—by faith. "Now faith has come, we are no longer under the supervision of the law" (Galatians 3:25). The law no longer babysits us. Does this mean we can do whatever we want? No. It means, because I live for God, my heart is to please God and my battle is with my flesh—not my Creator. There is no longer a division between you and me and our God. He is with us. Christ has made a way for us to God and we will not be kept from him ever. By the gift of faith, we realize that God's love for us came in the person of Jesus Christ to bring us back to himself—not by law—but by love. Love in you and me for him is the gift! We want to live for him from now on. Please read Romans 6, 7, and 8 with your question about your life in Christ, because truly that is what this question boils down to. And as you read, listen for God's love, blessing, provision, and purpose over your life.

> For if you live according to the sinful nature, you will die, but if by the Spirit you put to death the misdeeds of the body, you will live. For those who are led by the Spirit of God are the children of God. The Spirit you received does not make you slaves, so that you live in fear again; rather, the Sprit you received brought about your adoption to sonship. And by him we cry, 'Abba, Father'. The Spirit himself testifies with our spirit that we are God's children.
>
> Romans 8:13-16

And back to Galatians, because we have one God with one message—he is consistent.

> But if you are led by the Spirit, you are not under the law. The acts of the sinful nature are obvious. Sexual immorality, impurity and debauchery, idolatry and witchcraft; hatred, discord, jealousy, fits of rage, selfish ambition, dissensions, factions and envy; drunkenness, orgies and the like. I warn you—as I did before, that those who live like this will not inherit the kingdom of God.
>
> Galatians 5:18-21

Did you see the term "obvious"? That means you know it, and I know it—we all know what is wrong when the Spirit of God is telling us so clearly.

Let me stop for a moment and point out that indeed no specific examples are given for each outpouring of the sinful nature in Galatians 5:18-21. God will identify in us the specifics of how we each will carry them out—by his spirit. He will lovingly, graciously draw our attention to a pitfall to protect us, and help us remain in his love. And that is exactly what he is doing with you!

And I have to continue with Galatians 5:22-23 (with my commentary in parenthesis) and then I'll let you go talk with God on your own "But the fruit of the Spirit (those beautiful, healthy, life-giving drippings of goodness hanging off the vine that is our Savior!) is love, joy, peace, patience, kindness, goodness, faithfulness, gentleness and self-control. Against such (that means with these incredible spirit-given treasures) there is no law (This means that you can have at these natures that God will evoke in you! Have at 'em allllll you want!)." Do you want to know why there is no law against these things? Because they are not selfish acts; they are selfless. These are gifts in us to extend toward others as much as we want. Self is not the recipient, however by extending these gifts we are richly blessed. Are you hearing me?

Do not be deceived. Life in Christ is freedom from every sin that so easily entangles. The first clue that you are being deceived is your restlessness. How do you feel about masturbating? Guilt. That's not you, that's not your mom, that's not this culture—because you're fine according to the world's standards, sweet one. Instead, that's God in you. The second clue that you are being deceived is that your actions are self-driven, and you are trying to convince yourself otherwise. And finally, you know you are being deceived when your actions are opposed to God's Word. "'I have the right to do anything,' you say—but not everything is beneficial. 'I have the right to do anything'—but I will be mastered by nothing…The body is not meant for sexual immorality but for the Lord, and the Lord for the body" (1 Corinthians 6:12–13).

Let God teach you as you study his Word what that freedom from guilt feels like. Let God teach you what purity looks like. His Word gives clear instruction. Hear God's Word over every other influence in your life. "So whether you eat or drink, whatever you do, do it all for the glory of God" (1 Corinthians 10:31).

When we who love God seek ourselves over him we will sense the uncomfortable disconnect between the Spirit of God and our flesh. Thank God for that! When we who love God seek him, and fight the longings of our flesh so that we can abide in him constantly, we will have the gratifying peace of his spirit that passes all worldly understanding (Philippians 4:6-9).

Sex and the pleasures we have from it—all aspects of it—were not designed for self, but for God's glory in marriage. One man, with one woman; a union instituted by God in the Garden of Eden. "For this reason a man will leave his father and mother and be united to his wife and they will become one flesh. The man and his wife were both naked, and they felt no shame." (Genesis 2:24)

Not self-oriented pleasure. Each for the other. No shame.

I'd like to suggest Kay Arthur's book, *The Truth About Sex*. This is an incredible study about God's amazing design of sex in marriage. I trust he will teach you freeing truth as you seek him and his image of holiness in your life.

> The Spirit of the Lord is on me, because he has anointed me to proclaim good news to the poor. He has sent me to proclaim freedom for the prisoners and recovery of sight for the blind, to set the oppressed free, to proclaim the year of the Lord's favor.
>
> Luke 4:18-19

We are free!

Love!
Laura

Selected Scripture:

Study method:

Truth learned:

Steps I will take to apply it:

My message concerning "Freedom from Guilt":

GUARDED HEART WITH GUYS

DEAR LAURA,
I have this uncontrollable guard up to every guy I meet. I find myself being attracted to a guy, one who is really great and loves the Lord immensely, but the minute I see any sort of attraction from them towards me, I freak out and cut them off. I get scared or weirded out. It drives me crazy!! And the thing is, I am sooo bad at communicating my feelings to guys, so it makes things even more confusing and frustrating! How do I sort out my emotions with this, as well as being able to communicate them?

Reply:

Hey! Thanks for your question! Have you ever heard the saying, "Once bitten, twice shy"? That might be you, my friend. Have you been hurt in a relationship before? That might be the reason you are "freaking out" when you see that there may be mutual feelings between you and this fortunate young man. Here's a story for you. I remember when I first got braces on my teeth; I was so excited about them! I smiled constantly! I know that's very odd, but for some reason I really did like them. However, my affection for them did not last. It was not long before a 7th grade boy, whom I absolutely adored, told me that I looked funny with my braces. Of course, I cried. And, from then on, I hated my braces. Every time I smiled or laughed, no matter who was looking at me, I covered my mouth. It became a reflex habit that was extremely hard to break even when the braces were long gone. Sometimes I still catch myself doing it!

So what does that have to do with your question? Please know I am proceeding with much caution. Okay? I think that you are protecting yourself from being hurt, and I also think, to some degree, that is very wise. We should be careful about who we are close to. I love Psalm 1! God teaches us not to listen to the advice of people who do not love God, and not to hang out with people who are locked into sin as their way of life. The Bible tells us to get wisdom, and though it might cost all you have, get understanding (Proverbs 4). God's Word is full of wisdom that we can plug into our everyday situations, our relationships, and our purpose.

What you need when you are on the cusp of a new relationship is wisdom. And wisdom is not based on feeling; wisdom is based on truth. You may have fears that have a basis to them, and so when you are holding back, ask yourself why? Press the reasons for your fear up against truth—God's Word—to discern your steps, whether you move forward in the relationship or not. You may have fears that have no basis. You know what I mean? Like me with my braces—I covered my smile no matter who was looking at me, when it was really only one person that hurt my feelings. I didn't have to be afraid of everybody looking at my grin. I allowed that one person's cruelty to impact the way I felt and acted for two years of my life! You may have good reasons for why you are not sure of moving forward with the relationship, so let your caution be the yellow light that allows you time to pause, pray, and seek God about your concerns.

1. Pause.
2. Pray.
3. Find God's viewpoint in Scripture.

A dating relationship is nothing to go charging into recklessly. I love that you are being cautious. I think that's brilliant! And besides that—and this is just my opinion—I think a woman's heart is to be pursued, and a wise woman never lets that adventure end for the one she allows to catch her. As far as past hurts go, let them go. They are in the past. Move forward with the wisdom that you can glean from them as you learn God's Word and his amazing love for you. Remember that all things will work together for good to those who love God and are called according to his purpose (Romans 8:28). It is so, so true. Ask him to heal you and make those scars his glory. And how beautiful, sweet girl—as only he can make things beautiful—how beautiful his glory in you will be!!!

Thank you, thank you for writing to me!!!

Love!!!
Laura

Selected Scripture:

Study method:

Truth learned:

Steps I will take to apply it:

My message concerning "Guarded Heart with Guys":

HEART SAVIOR

Two different letters. Two different women.
One heart issue. One Savior.

DEAR LAURA,
Question 1: I have this problem of getting emotionally attached to guys very quickly. I always end up crushed and my heart destroyed because they leave or go after another girl. I know that I am to guard my heart and I try so hard to but, either I'm not doing the right thing or not trying hard enough. Because in the end, I get the same result—emotional attachment and a broken heart. I really would like practical ways to guard my heart and possibly a vivid picture of what a woman guarding her heart looks like when she interacts with guys. Thank you for listening.

Dear Laura,
Question 2: I have been so hurt and taken advantage of by guys in the past. It took me a long time to gain a man's trust back and now that I'm finally getting there, and have met awesome Christian guy friends who truly care about and support me as a sister in Christ, I struggle with how much is too much in opening my heart to them. In the past I didn't guard my heart but now I

feel like my heart is a steel wall. I am so scared of self-disclosing myself and placing myself in a vulnerable position, because I am so used to getting hurt and I've almost become numb to the pain. I am at a place now where I am totally pursuing God, waiting patiently, and trusting that his timing is the absolute best. At the same time, however, I'm not quite sure what a girl-guy friendship is supposed to look like. How much should we open our heart to them, and have it be in a healthy way? Also, what does it look like to be content in Christ alone? Will I still have that attraction to another person, even if I know that God wants me to be single in this time right now in my life??

Reply:

Hey! Thanks for writing to me! I love living out our faith with you girls! Love it! Both of these questions came around the same time—within days of each other—so I thought I would write to you both at the same time. You both have been hurt by guys in the past, and both of you refer to guarding your heart, wanting to know what that looks like as a young, single woman.

I am so excited about what God has in store for us to learn together! If you don't have your Bible right there with you, will you grab it so you can think about some Scripture with me? God's Word is our guide! Thank you for this opportunity to share this lesson with you.

Turn to Proverbs 4. I love the book of Proverbs. It was authored by our God, penned by King Solomon, son of King David. My study Bible explains that Proverbs provides instruction on how to live wisely and successfully in "the fear of the Lord." Fear of the Lord is reverence for, trust, and commitment to the Lord and his will. If you have a study Bible, it may say much of the same.

Both of you use the statement "guarding your heart" that is mentioned in Proverbs 4:23, "Above all else, guard your heart, for everything you do flows from it." We need to carefully examine the context of this instruction when we think about applying it to our lives. In order to understand a verse's meaning, we need to back up the inspection lens through which we are reading and look at the backdrop surrounding this verse. In other words, study the context of the verse. Take a minute with me and go back to the beginning of Proverbs 4. I'm going to type it out here for us, okay?

> Listen, my sons, to a father's instruction; pay attention and gain understanding. I give you sound learning, so do not forsake my teaching. For I, too, was a son to my father, still tender, and cherished by my mother. Then he taught me, and he said to me, 'Take hold of my words with all your heart; keep my commands, and you will live. Get wisdom, get understanding; do not forget my words or turn away from them. Do not forsake wisdom, and she will protect you. The beginning of wisdom is this: Get wisdom. Though it cost all you have, get understanding. Cherish her and she will exalt you; embrace her, and she will honor you. She will give you a garland to grace your head and present you with a glorious crown.' Listen my son, accept what I say, and the years of your life will be many. I instruct you in the way of wisdom and lead you along straight paths. When you walk, your steps will not be hampered; when you run, you will not stumble. Hold on to instruction, do not let it go; guard it well, for it is your life. Do not set foot on the path of the wicked or walk in the way of evildoers. Avoid it, do not travel on it; turn from it and go your way. For they cannot rest until they do evil; they are robbed of sleep till they make someone stumble. They eat the bread of wickedness and drink the wine of violence. The path of the righteous is like the morning sun, shining ever brighter till the full light of day. But the way of the wicked is like deep darkness; they do not know what makes them stumble. My son, pay attention to what I say; turn your ear to my words. Do not let them out of your sight; keep them within your heart, for they are life to those who find them

and health to one's whole body. Above all else guard your heart, for everything you do flows from it.

Proverbs 4:1-23

Okay, so we've landed on the verse that began our journey through Proverbs 4. "Above all else guard your heart, for everything you do flows from it." What do you think Solomon meant for his sons to understand about this? Before you answer, think about every verse that came before, and now read with me a little bit after that verse.

Keep your mouth free from perversity; keep corrupt talk from your lips. Let your eyes look straight ahead; fix your gaze directly before you. Give careful thought to the paths of your feet and be steadfast in all your ways. Do not turn to the right or the left; keep your foot from evil.

Proverbs 4:24-27

That's all 27 verses of Proverbs 4. So how are you doing with my question about the verse about guarding your heart? What can we understand about what this means? What it looks like? There is a cross-reference in my Bible to 2 Kings 10:31, and it is about Jehu, who was anointed King of Israel. Jehu was not careful to keep the law of the Lord with all his heart. He was not careful to turn from sin and because he would not live for God his entire kingdom suffered.

Jesus speaks from the wisdom in this verse in Luke 6:45, "Good people bring good things out of the good stored up in their heart, and evil people bring evil things out of the evil stored up in their heart. For out of the overflow of the heart the mouth speaks."

This guard for our heart, girls, is God's Word—God's instruction and wisdom. This guard over our heart is you and I keeping God's Word in—and sin out. Guarding your heart is not putting up a wall between you and a guy. Relationships require wisdom. Knowing who to spend time with, who to share life with, and what that looks like requires guidance from God, and he is the one who gives wisdom. So when you ask, "what does it look like to guard your heart?", consider from Proverbs 4 that this instruction is about getting wisdom from God, holding to his Word, and keeping your life free of anything evil.

We can absolutely apply that idea to relationships, as far as considering whether or not the relationship honors God. We can ask ourselves questions like: Is it wise to be in this relationship? Does this person honor me and my relationship with God? Does my boyfriend seek to protect my purity and my integrity? What are my motives for being with this person? What will the progression of this relationship look like? Does that picture honor and glorify God? These questions embody guarding your heart as it relates to Proverbs 4.

When you consider going on a date with someone (yes—even one date!!!), be very wise about who this person is and why you would want to venture into a relationship with him. Is he a follower of Christ? Does he demonstrate a love for God and others above a love for himself? Is he someone who you can respect? Why? What are those reasons? A guy worth your time should be a whole lot more than a nice shirt and great hair. And if that's all you know at the point when he is asking you out, my suggestion is to say no. This is guarding your heart.

You don't know him well enough to go out on a date with him. You might say, "Well how am I supposed to get to know him?" Glad you asked! That's his problem! Let him pursue you! My sweet husband pursued me three months before he asked me out on a first date! Three months!!! I still tease him about that, but I most certainly respected him for it.

The dating scene has changed so much, ladies. Wow! Casual cups of coffee here and there are cause for concern, girls. For a woman, I don't care how casual the date, we always have a heart attachment. Will he like me? Does he find me beautiful? Will he think my goals are interesting (you do have goals right?)? Will he ask me out again? There's nothing casual about those feelings. The way to avoid that kind of hurt is to avoid that kind of dating pattern. Know his intentions, and do not be a time-filler, lonely-night, last-minute "come-to-the-rescue-of-this-poor-lonely-heart" kind of girl. Do not put yourself in those casual situations. Have enough respect for yourself to put up a white picket fence around your dating life.

Check out these great books: *And the Bride Wore White* by Dannah Gresh, *Passion and Purity* by Elizabeth Elliot, *Ending the Search for Mr. Right* by Michelle McKinney Hammond. Ladies, I realize that you can get your feelings hurt even if this person you go out with is someone you have known and hung out with as friends; even if you have the guidelines set up, relationships still crash and burn. Let's face it, you can't always avoid pain when you venture into a relationship. However, you can avoid being disrespected as a woman who loves and lives for God. Hold on to God's Word. Get wisdom. Proverbs 4 is all about avoiding what is evil and clinging to the Word of God which is the guard that will keep you from shame and guilt. So the relationship wasn't right. Let it end in a dignified manner. Trust God with the direction he has given you, and move on.

Philippians 4:6-7 gives us huge direction that I hope encourages you. "Do not be anxious about anything, but in every situation, by prayer and petition, with thanksgiving, present your requests to God. And the peace of God, which transcends all understanding, will guard your hearts and your minds in Christ Jesus."

Love!!!

Laura

Selected Scripture:

Study method:

Truth learned:

Steps I will take to apply it:

My message concerning "Heart Savior":

HE LOVES YOU

DEAR LAURA,

I have been saved since I was a child and grew up in a Christian home. I am surrounded by people who know the Lord, and I often question where I stand in my walk with Christ. I read in my Christian books and devotionals that being a Christian isn't just about listening to the right music, reading your Bible from time to time, hanging out with good people and not partying. It's more than that—it's about truly knowing who Christ is and loving him with a devoted heart. I get so pumped up when I go to Christian events or church services where the Word of God is proclaimed so loud and boldly in my face—but then when the excitement fades, I feel like my passion for the Lord fades. I walk in and out of having a passionate heart for him and sometimes I wonder if I really accepted him into my heart at all. I have rededicated my life to Christ before but still messed up after that—it seems like I just can't get my relationship right with him. My life doesn't prove at all that I have stepped over the line and am willing to embrace Christ with wherever he leads me. I get so frustrated because I want to love Jesus so deeply—I want him to be the only thing that matters. I am sick of caring about what others think and what this world wants me to be.

I feel like lately I have been challenged so much with hearing about stories how people have recommitted their lives to Christ and have crossed that line where they surrender all of themselves to Christ. I want to be there. I want to trust him with everything I have in me. There is so much that I feel like I don't trust God with—not because I don't want to but maybe because I just don't know how. I want to know what I am truly living for. I don't want to be afraid of this life, and I don't want to question my walk with him anymore. What more can I do in my life that will give me solitude and stability in my life with Christ? Is it normal to question this, or am I really not believing the things that I claim to live for? I want to be in love with my Savior—I want what I see others have with him!

Reply:

Hey, Sweet One! Thanks for emailing me! I am so glad to have a chance to talk to you! Please know I am praying and seeking God with every word I type. Your heart is precious to him—and to me—and so I speak most carefully and with God's Word as my guide. I will only ever direct you to his Word and to him. Okay? That being said, I want to point out something critical in what you wrote to me. Here it is: "I get so pumped up when I go to Christian events or church services where the Word of God is proclaimed so loud and boldly in my face—but then when the excitement fades, I feel like my passion for the Lord fades. I walk in and out of having a passionate heart for him and sometimes I wonder if I really accepted him into my heart at all."

Sweet girl, you have identified quite clearly the issue of your concern...feeling. You get pumped...and then the excitement fades. Then you wonder about what really happened between you and Jesus—simply because the feeling is gone. My dear friend, there is nothing about our relationship with Christ that should hinge on feeling. If you live for God based on your feelings, you will be like a wave on the sea tossed this way and that (James

1:2-5). Believe and do not doubt despite circumstances in your life—whether they are good circumstances, or bad ones. By faith we accept him—and by obedience to his Word we live for him. Love for God and from God has never been about feeling. The joy we experience is absolutely a blessing that comes from loving God, but that happy feeling falsely defines true love and that happy feeling is false security for a loving relationship.

Please allow me to explain...but only after I digress for momentary trip down memory lane. I remember very vividly, when I was fourteen, I told a boy that I loved him. He, being older and wiser at fifteen (ha!), said to me, "What constitutes your love for me?" Wow! Not the response I was expecting, but definitely one I would never forget. I had no idea what he had just asked because at fourteen the word "constitutes" sounded like something I wasn't supposed to do or talk about. Unfortunately I have no idea what my answer was in that intensely confusing moment, but I do remember that I would have rather died than let on to the fact that I had no clue what he was asking me. However, now that I am much older, I most certainly know I would have not had an impressive answer for him even if I did understand the word "constitutes." Because the fact of the matter was I didn't understand love or what ingredients should "make up or found"—constitute—my love for anyone at fourteen or at any age.

So, can I ask you something? What constitutes your love for God? And, do you know what constitutes his love for you? These are two very separate and critical questions to consider as we approach your concerns and the Word of God. Think about God's depiction of love for us in the Bible. Take his love for Israel for example. His love for his people is constant—despite how they made him feel...which for the most part was angry. He never let them go and gave them a savior because of his commitment to them, to us, to those who would believe by faith and not feeling. If feelings brought us to our commitment to Christ, then feelings will easily take us from him as well. We as believers are to walk by faith in who God says he is. How critical it is then to get into God's Word and spend time with him to get to know him—his promises, his instruction. Feelings could (will) get in the way of that every day, couldn't they (won't they)?

Hebrews 11! Will you check out this passage of Scripture? Really read it carefully and ask yourself how each person highlighted in this chapter might have felt while they were doing—by faith—what pleased God...because my guess is their actions went hard core against their feelings. There is no way Noah felt like building an ark in the desert. There is no way Abraham felt like sacrificing his son Isaac. There is no way Joshua felt like marching around an entire city seven times. These people and others mentioned in Hebrews 11 acted on one thing: faith.

Faith in God is a gift that brings us to greater understanding of who he is; faith helps us seek and hope in his promises; faith stirs us to boldly defining acts of obedience, gratitude, and the realization of his love, and not necessarily in that order.

I would love for you to read Ann Voskamp's book *One Thousand Gifts*. She has eloquently scripted what it is to live by faith and not by feeling. Feelings ebb and flow in moments that God gives, and we are deceived when we buy into the idea that a feeling constructed in beautiful circumstances was the presence of God. God is always present. Will we see him in every moment, or miss him because our senses have been tuned for pleasure and not for the glory of God? When the worship service ends, your experience with God does not. He dwells in you. He is always with you. Your life, dear heart, is a worship service.

You believe in God. Yes? You made a commitment to live for Christ. Correct? You love him, because he first loved you; am I right? Are you now living out your belief? Are you living out your love for God? Don't just answer yes. Examine your life and the decisions you make carefully. Are you studying God's Word to know him—to understand his instruction for your life in him? Are you then living out of what you learn and realize about God?

Seeking him for what his Word should look like in your skin? Knowing our God and living out his Word is actually what it means to be bathed in the source of love in our life (John 14 and 15). Consider Christ—he is the perfect model for how we are to live. Everything he did demonstrated his love for the Father and his love for others. Please take time and read John 14 and 15. Please?

Love from God and love for God is not a mushy, gushy, sweep you off your feet kind of feeling. God did not define love for him this way in Scripture.

> Jesus replied, 'Anyone who loves me will obey my teaching. My Father will love them and we will come to them and make our home with them. Anyone who does not love me will not obey my teaching. These words you hear are not my own; they belong to the Father who sent me.'
>
> John 14:23-24

> As the Father has loved me, so have I loved you. Now remain in my love. If you keep my commands, you will remain in my love, just as I have kept my Father's commands and remain in his love. I have told you this so that my joy may be in you and that your joy may be complete.
>
> John 15:9-11

"Greater love has no one than this: to lay down one's life for one's friends" (John 15:13).

"For God so loved the world, that he gave his only Son..." (John 3:16a).

Love requires the sacrifice of one's feelings—one's will. Joy is a product of love.

When we realize this truth that Jesus is teaching us about the source of love that is ours to realize, then any emotional feeling about our God will have deep roots; roots that grow daily out of an intimate connection with God through his Word, blossoming our faith and motivating our obedience.

Live by God's Word and let him be master of your feelings. What would that look like? Oh my goodness if we—together— would daily reject fear, discomfort, doubt, pride, greed, impurity, lust, anger, rage, malice, lies, filthy language, gossip, slander, envy, our own understanding—and live as God's chosen people, holy and dearly loved…can you even imagine it? Can we be that? It's what we were called to be. We must be able. Check out Colossians 1:9-14, Colossians 3:1-17! Truth to hold on to, encourage others with, and live!

One thing I hope you embrace most assuredly as I close is the truth that God loves you! In our sins Christ died for us. Wow!!! Such love! God loves you! No matter if you live for him or not, he loves you! He loves the world! He died for all of us, and the Bible teaches our actions do not determine his love. We often mistake his love with his blessing. When we walk in the fountain of his love (living for him in obedience to his Word), we walk in his blessing. Total difference. John 14 and 15 make this most clear to me. We are one with the Father because of Christ—believe it and live out of it. Feelings cannot change such a truth—or ever fully express it.

Will you pray with me God's Word from Ephesians 3:16-19? I pray that out of your glorious riches, Lord, you may strengthen us with power through your spirit in our inner being, so that Christ may dwell in our hearts through faith. And I pray that we being rooted and established in love, may have power together with all your people, God, to grasp how wide and long and high and deep is the love of Christ, and to know this love that sur- passes knowledge—that we may be filled to the measure of all the fullness of you our God. Amen!

Love!
Laura

Selected Scripture:

Study method:

Truth learned:

Steps I will take to apply it:

My message concerning "He Loves You":

LIMITLESS BEAUTY

HI, LAURA
I recently got engaged, and through this engagement God has been opening my eyes to a lot of sin in my life. I'm overwhelmed by the number of idols I see in my heart. The one I am battling with most to gain a godly perspective on is working out. I want my fiancé to think I am beautiful; I want to please him. I know this is not a struggle that has just all of a sudden come up. I have struggled with wanting to have a perfect body, with wanting to have a perfect image for some time now. I know that working out in itself is not sin, but my reaction to it is sin, because I place too much of my security and too much of my identity on how I look and how good my fiancé thinks I look.

He is a godly man, and he has told me countless times that what attracts him to me most is Christ in me, yet I still struggle with a standard of beauty that I create for myself in terms of weight. I enjoy working out; I want to be healthy, but more than anything I want to be a godly wife who finds her all in Christ. In order to do that, I know in my head I need to be hard on any sin God reveals, but my wicked heart wants to justify this sin by telling me I only have a few months to get in tip top shape before the wedding. Any advice you have would be greatly appreciated.

Thank you!

Reply:

Oh my friend! Sit down here, next to me a sec...Let me hold your hand tightly. You with me? I'm lookin' at ya lovingly eye to eye, heart to heart, girl to girl. It's okay I call myself a girl still, right? I'm in the autumn of my life as I write this to you, but even so, like you, I battle with the way I look, and I will continue to fight for health and beauty that will sustain this shell, and not just for my man—who still reaches for me after all these years—but for my babes, who currently at ten and eight look up to me and still want to be held on my hip even if just to make them laugh. And a good laugh we all have!

Congratulations on your engagement! What a beautiful gift from God! How exciting that you have found a mate for life! One that you will laugh with, cry with, spend hours upon countless hours growing old with, growing wise with, growing more in love with. One that you will see the world with, and one whose life you will witness, and one who will in turn witness your own: a help mate! Never again will it just be you and God, but you and God and your mate. A man that you will have to love, more than you love yourself; one man that you will have to forgive more than you have ever forgiven anyone or anything; one man that you will have to embrace when you do not feel like hugging. As a wife you will do life with one man by whom you will honor God in every act of submission—in every "yes" that you would rather be a "no", of your giving when you would rather withhold, and in your withholdings when you would rather let him have it!

You will learn to ignore dirty socks, bad breath, messy toilets, and all before the night air of romance, and candles, and perfume rests on your pillow. You will learn to sit beside him in vomit—either your own or his—along with debt, due dates, and job hunts or job burdens. You will learn to deny your own desires so that he can have. You will enjoy moments so delirious with stress that prayers will overflow from tears, and you won't be able to discern whose tears belong to whom.

You will want to know his pain, and not just his physical pain but his spiritual pain. And you will want him to know yours, and then you will learn only God can feel it and take it for either of you. You will want for him to realize your every dream, and facilitate it moment by longing-filled moment. Then you will come to understand with struggle or maybe, by grace, you will learn with ease, that only God was meant to bear the burden of your dreams. And for God alone that burden is great joy. Congratulations sweet girl, you have chosen to embrace a man for life. One that you will have to feed more than food, more than water, but one that you will get to feed the Word of God as he comes alongside of you for encouragement, hope, and strength!

Congratulations on finding that one person whom God will use in your life, not only to encourage you in what it looks like to love without condition but also to sharpen you with stone and steel for what it looks like to live in skin filled by Jesus. Congratulations on having the courage to enter a refining pot that is a fire unlike any other furnace, challenge, or race you will ever know or want to know. It is a journey toward holiness that only God can secure, that only God's Word can bless and fortify. And oh how he does it! And oh my soul, how does he do it?

Marriage is a marathon that few finish, be it because of pain, boredom, stress, lack of luster, creativity, self-discipline, lack of loyalty—or simply just because it wasn't what they thought it was going to be. I can promise you this my friend, as I have run this course now since 1998, I have never longed for God more, and have never seen him so beautifully. I haven't had to look far for him either—only to my side where my spouse runs beside me holding tightly to the hand of our God. Yes, I am crying. And yes, this is why some women cry at weddings, these reasons and a thousand other reasons of life and love that you will have the joy to discover with one man.

Congratulations! So, how are your abs now? Not even a thought, right? I don't mean to be hard on you. Truly. I am grateful for your words, for the reminder of where I have been and for where I could be in a moment even today. I am a woman. And I will always be that. Like you though, I love Jesus, and like you I refuse to be a woman who lives for any other god.

I remember shopping for my wedding gown with the very same thoughts you are having today. And as you said, wanting to be beautiful for him is not sin. But also as you have so wisely stated, what we do with that desire can in fact become a big, fat idol that is so hard to carry—and one that we were never meant to lug around.

I always want my husband to look to me and desire me. I will work hard to stay strong, healthy and desirable for the man God gave me to love. But beauty has limitations. It can't, nor was it ever meant to be everything. Your physical beauty will indeed bring pleasure...but it can never bring joy. Joy is something that is far, far, deeper. Joy is more lasting, more real. Joy can be felt in plenty and in want, in sickness and in health; it can be felt in the skinny of your workout power moments and the plump of your possible post-partum slump. Joy can be found in the creases of your marriage wrinkles and the scars of your heart, and it is absolutely in the freshness and lightness of your youth. Joy is beyond the exterior—always. Joy is the work of the Spirit of God.

What I have come to realize, not by ease—not ever by ease for me—is that I can miss joy when I am consumed with myself. When your fiancé tells you that you are beautiful, do you say: "Thank you." Or do you begin to think: "What must I do to remain like this? What do I have on that I can repeat? What must I do tomorrow to maintain what he sees?" Do you go there in your thoughts? Ugh! The agony of that drill!

"To all perfection I see a limit, but your commands are boundless" (Psalm 119:96).

This writer—probably well acquainted with beauty—knew with his heart where beauty dwells...God's Word! Woman, we must pursue that beauty with all of our efforts that are wasted on skin and hair and clothing. So what does that look like, right? Where is the balance of being healthy and beautiful without carting around an Aphrodite idol? Ask God! He is directing your heart always. You sense what a sickness to your spiritual health is right now. You already know sumpthin' just ain't right. God will teach you truth in his Word to help you realize what a beauty regime in your God-lovin' life is. He will teach you the full life you were meant to realize every single day. Daily go to his Word, wrap it around your heart and mind, and live it out as he teaches it to you. Go with him to the places in your mind where you are uncertain of your behavior, and ask him to examine it. We need his Word to do this, because our own way of thinking is never correct (see Proverbs 3:6).

I do work out. I want to be strong and healthy. However, I do not ever want to spend more time on the exterior than I do on the heart of this temple. And that "time" does not only include work out time but also thought time. Ouch. We need to train ourselves to take captive every thought of "me" and to consider the heart in front of us—to see him, to see her without seeing ourselves in front of them.

My dear friend, I know you know this. From the heart, everything we are overflows. We don't want that overflow to be the gutter slop of self. We want that overflow to be the fountain beauty of God's truth. It will gleam from our eyes and glisten on our lips before a world we get to love! And oh girl it will wash over our husbands! What beauty your husband will get to lavish in!

Please do not get discouraged in your struggle to level an idol. I'm so excited for you!! I mean so few of us are brave enough, strong enough, and humble enough to admit our struggles. So thank you! Your struggle in itself is beautiful. That is God's glory in you busting to shine through.

Look around you, my friend, and pray for the women who are with you. See them. Encourage them with the truths you are learning about the beauty that is God's Word. The Word of God is limitless—inexhaustible—never fading—and free. But God's Word is not for the weak hearted. It will work you out! Hard! I'm talkin' resurrection Jesus hard (See Colossians 1-3)! God's Word is beautiful, and powerful, and it will not fail anyone who wants to be trained by it to level Aphrodite, or any other idol for that matter. Come on with that, Wonder Woman! Battle on!

Enjoy your engagement days. Ask God for what he would have you learn. Maybe consider one word to study and focus on as you prepare to be a wife—as you prepare to love one man. A word like heart, or beauty, or joy, or witness: look in your concordance and see where God will lead you. For life, oh my heart, go to his Word to learn and grow and beautify the creation that is you for the rest of your life!

"Your statutes are my heritage forever. They are the joy of my heart. My heart is set on keeping your decrees to the very end" (Psalm 119:11-12).

Love!

Laura

P.S. Some pre-marriage reading suggestions: *For Women Only* by Shaunti Feldhaun, *The Power of a Praying Wife* by Stormie Omartian, *Counterfeit Gods* by Tim Keller, *Love as a Way of Life* by Gary Chapman (author of *The Five Love Languages*—also great!), *So Long Insecurity* by Beth Moore, and *Lord, Only You Can Change Me* by Kay Arthur. Those should keep ya busy for a while. Don't forget to breathe between the lines, and know I'm reading and studying with you!

Selected Scripture:

Study method:

Truth learned:

Steps I will take to apply it:

My message concerning "Limitless Beauty":

LADY-IN-WAITING

DEAR LAURA,
As I was reading what Kemper has written to the guys, I came across, "We, as men, were created to rescue, to pursue, to provide for." I also agree with this statement, whether-old fashioned or not, that men always do the pursuing. The fall of Adam and Eve does come to mind when thinking about men as the providers. Is there any Scripture that explains how a woman should be in fact treated and the roles of her man in pursuing her heart?

Reply:

Hey, Sweet Girl! Thank you for writing! Most of these words I have gathered for this response will not be my own (which is always a good thing). I would like to reference some amazing authors that will help us discover truth.

Your question is answered best in the book of Ruth. Ruth is the perfect model of a woman who is completely dependent on God for meeting her needs. She pursued God first, and he provided for her, beyond her happily-ever-after dreams. Ruth is the epitome—the very God-authored image—of the "lady in waiting". Listen to what Boaz says to her when he comes to profess his devotion:

Then he said, 'May you be blessed of the Lord, my daughter. You have shown your last kindness to be better than the first by not going after young men, whether poor or rich. Now, my daughter, do not fear. I will do for you whatever you ask, for all my people in the city know that you are a woman of excellence.'

Ruth 3:10-11

In the book *Lady in Waiting*, best-selling author and speaker, Jackie Kendall, draws her readers into God's book—specifically, the book of Ruth. She explains:

Ruth, single, young, widowed—must have experienced the lonely longings for the warmth of a husband. But she lived in victory over her desire to 'man hunt'. Instead of 'going after the boys,' she sat still and let God bring her prince to her. She was a Lady of Security. Why do women tend to 'go after the guys'? Why do women experience difficulty being still and waiting for the man to initiate and develop the relationship? You find the answer in one word: insecurity. An insecure woman has her world centered on something (marriage) or someone (Mr. Right) that can be taken away. Insecurity keeps a woman from experiencing consistent joy even within a relationship because a man cannot provide security, only God can.

(Kendall et al, 1995)

Here's something else Jackie wrote for us to consider:

Why do women feel they have to go after men? Many women have believed a lie. They think, 'I must get the best for myself because God may not give it to me.' What do you think would have been the outcome of Ruth's life if she had chosen to believe this lie?

(Kendall et al, 1995)

Now, in order to answer that, you need to read the book of Ruth. So, please, please, take some time with your heavenly Daddy who wants you to know his heart—not just this story—and read this book. And, sweet girl, don't just read it to get through it like a novel. Pray first. Ask God to open your heart and your mind to teach you what he would have you learn. Take a pen in hand and have it ready to write out what you are thinking, learning, or questioning. Use God's Word to direct you deeper into what you are learning. I'm hoping you have a study Bible with a concordance and cross-references that will take you deeper into the Bible and all God is showing you in the book you will be studying.

To illustrate the depth and breadth of God's Word and how it unlocks more than what is seen or can be understood on the surface of one passage, consider Ruth 4:18-22 which lists the descendants of Ruth. She married the man God brought to her, Boaz. They had children together, and these descendants are all listed in the last verses of this chapter. Now, if I just read this book as a normal textbook, I might skip over those names and not think much of them except that it's nice she had kids and grandkids, and wow those names are hard to say. But, since this book is the Word of God, we have to take note of cool stuff that we might miss if we didn't consider it as God's book. This book is unlike any other.

A study Bible is a fabulous tool that helps unlock some of those jewels that we might overlook. So, in my study Bible there is a note to go along with those verses that list the genealogy of Ruth. This note actually directs me to the book of Matthew where another genealogy is given—the genealogy of Christ. And low and behold—guess whose name is given? I'll quote it for you. First it says in Matthew 1:1 "This is the genealogy of Jesus the Messiah, the son of David, the son of Abraham." Then the following verses go from Abraham, and then a whole bunch of other names from the descendants of Abraham right down to verses 5-6 which say, "Salmon the father of Boaz the father of Obed, whose mother was Rahab, Boaz the father of Obed whose mother was Ruth, Obed the father of Jesse, and Jesse the father of King David." How's that for a happily-ever-after story? Ruth is the great grandmother of King David, and Jesus directly followed that lineage. Ruth is related to God's Son! We can't even imagine what God has in store for those of us who are obedient.

Allow me to share this passage from Jackie's book where she quotes Elizabeth Elliot the wife of missionary Jim Elliot and the author of *Passion and Purity* (another great book you may want to read!).

> Elizabeth Elliot says she is often asked the question, 'What can I do to get him to notice me?' Note carefully the advice she gives. 'My answer is nothing. That is, nothing toward the man. Don't call him. Don't write a little note with a smiley face, or a flower, or fish under the signature and put it in his campus mailbox. Don't slide up to him in the hall and gasp, "I've just got to talk to you!" Don't look woebegone, don't ignore him, don't pursue him, don't do him favors; don't talk about him to nine carefully selected listeners. There is one thing you can do: turn the whole business over to God. If he's the man God has for you, "No good thing does he withhold from those who walk uprightly" Psalm 84:11. Direct your energies to obedience, not to nailing the man. God has his own methods of getting the two of you together. He doesn't need any help or advice from you.'
>
> (Kendall et al, 1995)

What powerful advice! Pursue God. This is our model for how we are to live, love, exist. What a relief we can leave everything up to him! How good, how glorious, how amazing is our God! He does it all. He is all. Please, enjoy his story of Ruth, and please share with me what wondrous things you learn from and about him. Thank you for your question and this opportunity to learn with you on this journey we share!

Love,
Laura

Selected Scripture:

Study method:

Truth learned:

Steps I will take to apply it:

My message concerning "Lady in Waiting":

LATHER, RINSE, REPEAT

DEAR LAURA,
I guess this isn't really a question. It's a statement. I can't stop having sex with my boyfriend. I can't. I want to, but I can't. I feel bad. Then do it again. I tell him we can't. Then we do it again. I want to stop. It's just not happening. I'm sick of the cycle. I'm giving in to sex, because it's easier than living for Christ. I guess that's the bottom line. It's too hard to stop.

Reply:
That's one bold statement you're making. Shout it, sweet, sweet hurting heart, as loud and as long as you want to. I will listen to your hurt, your frustration, and your feelings of inadequacy. I will listen, but I will not let you walk away from me believing that lie. Your statement simply isn't true. Hear this loud and clear: You can stop. You can. You may be tempted by the very same sin until the day you die. But when it comes to sin—any sin—we who are indwelt by the Spirit of the living God—always have a choice, and we always have the power to choose freedom from sin.

Will you read Romans 8:1-9 with me? Get your Bible and turn to it with me. I want to show you something amazing that we need to grasp together. I'll wait. Go get it. We need God's

Word to wash over our wrong thinking in 2 Timothy 3:16-17 style! So, go get your copy of God's Word. I'll be here when you get back. And if you don't have a copy of God's Word, I'll type out the passage we will read together below. Let's check this out!

> Therefore there is now no condemnation for those who are in Christ Jesus, because through Christ Jesus the law of the Spirit who gives life has set you free from the law of sin and death. For what the law was powerless to do because it was weakened by the sinful nature, God did by sending his own Son in the likeness of sinful humanity to be a sin offering. And so he condemned sin in human flesh, in order that the righteous requirement of the law might be fully met in us, who do not live according to the sinful nature but according to the Spirit. Those who live according to the sinful nature have their minds set on what that nature desires; but those who live in accordance with the Spirit have their minds set on what the Spirit desires. The mind controlled by the sinful nature is death, but the mind controlled by the Spirit is life and peace. The sinful mind is hostile to God; it does not submit to God's law, nor can it do so. Those controlled by the sinful nature cannot please God. You, however, are not controlled by the sinful nature but are in the Sprit, if indeed the Spirit of God lives in you.
>
> Romans 8:1–9a

Let's study some of these verses together, okay. I'm so excited, I can hardly stand it! First, will you pray this with me? Father, we are grateful for your Word. We are grateful that you wrote it and have preserved it, protected it, and provided it here now so we can know you, the One in whom is all knowledge, wisdom, and understanding. Teach us please, God. Wash over our wrong thinking with truth, so we live differently for your amazing purpose in Christ. Thank you, Lord. We seek you, believing you are your Word. Amen!

Read the Romans 8:1-9 passage several times. Truly, reading the passage more than once is a great reading strategy! The first time you read a passage, it's like a drive by. You see color. The second time you read it, you recognize shapes. The third time you read the passage you should begin to discover meaning.

Identify the word for word truth in each verse. Now when you start to identify shapes, you are locking in on the truth in that verse. So, another reading strategy that we can apply to God's book is to think about the truth you have identified. A good way to think about that is to write it down. We're studying, right? When I study to know something, I take advantage of every opportunity God has given me to know him. So, low and behold, pen and paper lend themselves to knowing God. Hey, we use pen and paper to prepare for a job, to learn in school, to connect with others, so why wouldn't we use pen and paper or whatever tools available to learn of our God. So, let's write down the truth that we lock into as we read each verse.

Right off the starting block we have huge, refreshing truth. Do you see it in Romans 8:1? "Therefore, there is now no condemnation for those who are in Christ Jesus." What is the truth in those words? This may seem like a hard question, but we can answer it easily using the words on the page. Yup, you are simply restating what the passage already says.

Understand this truth: there is no condemnation for those who are in Christ Jesus. Do you know what condemnation means? Well, if we're not sure, we better be sure. God has it in there for us to realize. So, let's Google it. Okay, I found it. Condemnation is the process of pronouncing guilty. Does that make sense? In a court of law, following the judgment process, condemnation is sure. Guilt is established, and so a person is then condemned. What truth can we grab from this verse now that we understand condemnation? Can you think that through? There is now no condemnation. The penalty for the guilty verdict that we are due is not held against any of us who are in Christ Jesus.

Think about this truth. Meditate on it. Wow! Is that amazing or what? Okay if you're not finding that amazing, let's process this together. We're meditating on God's Word. This is meditating on truth! Consider all the sin you have committed in your entire life. Hard, right? It's immeasurable, isn't it? According to God's Word, our sin does not condemn us because we live in Jesus. Dear heart, when you stand before Jesus—the One who was tortured on a cross for your sin and mine so that we could be righteous before God the Father, we have no reputation of any of those past wrongs. Can you imagine that? And not only is our reputation righteous, we get to live in that righteous standing forever in his kingdom of love. Amazing!

As that truth sinks into your heart and mind, as only God's spirit is able to give the Word of God absorption in flesh, how does that make you feel about having sex with your boyfriend? For me, my sin only becomes more putrefying and my desire to run from it only intensifies. Why would we live for anything or anyone but Jesus?

We get lost in wrong thinking, don't we? We forget; this is why we need the Word of God before our eyes, embossing it by study onto our minds and by lifestyle deep in our hearts.

Living God's Word changes our heart. Did you hear that? You may learn it with your mind, but not until you live it will it become real in your heart. Do you believe according to the Word of God that Jesus of Nazareth is the Son of God, and that he has the power to save you from your life of sin?

"Jesus said to her, 'I am the resurrection and the life. Anyone who believes in me will live, even though they die; and whoever lives by believing in me will never die. Do you believe this?'" (John 11:25–26).

Believing this truth is critical, because believing God's Word changes everything about you from death to life. Knowing it is fruitless. Head knowledge of the Bible only increases your odds for winning a game of Bible Trivial Pursuit.

Add to your knowledge of God's Word the experiences of doing it (2 Peter 1:3-11). "For if you do these things, you will never stumble" 2 Peter 1:10b.

Consider the woman caught in the act of adultery in John 8. She was brought before Jesus to be accused, and condemned. She must have felt guilt, shame, embarrassment, completely mortified, and terrified. According to the Jewish legal system this woman's guilt condemned her to death by stoning. Fear for her life must have been overwhelming.

The woman's guilt was not in question; she was caught in the act. Jesus did not reiterate her guilt. In fact he did not say anything about what she already realized in her humiliating exposure. The sin factor did not need further explanation. This woman already knew the law—and she broke it anyway. She needed to learn something about the love of her God. Because God gave his Son, the adulteress would be free from condemnation.

Jesus said to her, "Go, and leave your life of sin" (John 8:11b).

This woman should have died, but she was set free. How do you think she lived from then on? Would she have run to her lover's bed? Jesus gave her back her life. He gave her freedom, and he gave her new direction. Even if she were tempted to return to her lover, out of love or habit, the words of Jesus would be with her always to remind her that she had been set free.

This truth is the same for you and me!! Christ does not accuse us nor condemn us to face what we deserve. In fact, while we were sinners, he died for us! Romans 5:8! In Jesus, we are not condemned. How we live in the light of that realization is up to us. Please hear me, okay? Jesus changed my view of my sin; Jesus came into my life as he did the life of this adulteress and, like her, he did not accuse me. He simply set me free.

What do you think the adulterous woman did after that moment with Jesus? Do you think she would return to her life of adultery? Or do you think she chose to follow Christ? Even though that encounter did not reveal the depths of his salvation, Jesus had given her freedom and direction through love, not condemnation. This woman must have been so pumped with the mercy extended toward her! I imagine she followed him; sought him out wherever he was, and if she didn't know where he was, she looked for him. I imagine she became the kind of Christ-follower that hung on every word and direction he gave. I imagine she followed him right to the foot of the cross, and cried in horror as she watched her Redeemer die, powerless to do for him what he had done for her. And I imagine this woman, clinging to those who mourned the crucified one, rejoiced with the news of his resurrection, and stood in awe with those who saw him ascend. What do you think she thought of her Savior then? What do you think she thought of her life of sin?

The Bible doesn't tell us what became of her, but it does draw us to consider our own lives—free from condemnation. How will we live from now on? Will you consider this with me? How will we live from now on, my friend?

How will this truth—that in Christ we are no longer condemned—come through our life? That answer is totally up to you. I can't answer it for you, nor could you answer it for me. Will you think about that for a moment—think about the truth God gave us and ask him to turn the light on in your heart with his love for you. Write down your thoughts. Yup. Back to pen and paper; these tools help us remember the truth we learned and how God, himself, impressed it on our hearts and minds.

I began with Romans 8:1-9, and in order to study all of it we have a lot more verses to go. We're not even on verse two yet! See how rich and full the Word is! I get so lost in the fullness of it! I lose track of time in it!

There are many other verses we could study and think about together, but I will let you go so you can study them on your own. I believe that God himself will speak to your heart more powerfully than I ever could. Your statement, that you cannot stop having sex with your boyfriend is not true. You can. You choose not to. The statement that you made that it is too hard to live for Jesus is broken thinking weighted down in continuous guilt-ridden choices. Jesus set you free from your sin and guilt. The choice to leave that life is yours because God Almighty gave it to you. Take that freedom, and walk in it one step at a time. Look forward so you do not stumble by constantly looking back. You won't look back at your prison of guilt when the kingdom of God is ever before you.

Here's that truth we have learned together:

1. You are free from condemnation in Christ.

2. God's love for us is not condemning, but life giving—new life with new direction out of love.

Sweet, sweet heart, what will it look like for you to leave your life of sin and live out God's love for you? Pray. Ask God to guide you. He will. Write down the action plan he gives you, and tell a Jesus-loving friend who will encourage you and walk with you as you live for God.

Wash your mind and heart in the truth of God's Word.

Rinse away the crippling guilt of your old life by doing what he has told you.

Repeat this process daily.

Love!
Laura

Selected Scripture:

Study method:

Truth learned:

Steps I will take to apply it:

My message concerning "Lather, Rinse, Repeat"

LONGING TO BE FILLED

DEAR LAURA,
I was reading your blog (www.laura-lewis.blogspot.com) about your struggles with an eating disorder. I am currently in the same boat. I binge eat all the time and I know I'm doing it to "fill" something but I don't know what I'm filling. I guess my question is, do you still struggle with food? Does the struggle ever go away or is it always there? Will I always feel the need to "fill" myself with something, whether it be binging or restricting food, self-medicating, or cutting? I don't want to deal with any of it anymore but it's always on my mind! Any words you can offer would be greatly appreciated! Thanks again for all your help as I begin a new, and to be honest scary, journey with God.

Reply:
My sweet friend! I am sorry you struggle with an eating disorder! Ugh! I know your frustration and it makes me ache with you! Literally! Before I get into the depth of our shared issue I want to first of all give you hope. We have a true God who will fill us so we are satisfied. Of this I am most certain, and because of this

I am excited for you to live anew through him! Keep that hope in mind as I answer your question. You ready for this?

You asked: Does the struggle ever go away or is it always there?

Answer: For me, the struggle never goes away. The draw to—and I do mean the draw—or in churchy terms, the "temptation" to return to the empty ways I used to gratify my flesh does not leave me. Why? Indeed, why! For some people, I know their old temptations are gone, but you know what? Glory to God for his purposes in each of his servants and for this girl, I can tell you, my struggle ain't over yet.

You also asked: Will I always feel the need to "fill" myself with something? I can't wait to answer that one. Hold please, and hear me out for a second.

Do I feel the weight of my temptation to binge and purge every moment of the day (or even every day)? No, not anymore. It does ease up the more disciplined I have become in fighting it and building up my strength to refuse to return to it (Isaiah 40:29). I cannot tell you the last time I binged and purged. It was a long, long time ago. Having held to a habit that (ridiculously) brought much comfort, it blows my mind that I am free from its eight year grip! The initial days of trying to follow God and not my temptation had lots of trip-ups along the way. I am grateful for the power of the Holy Spirit that will not let us rest—that will not let us quit—that teaches us to endure and grow through temptation (James 1:2, 3, 12)! I love the power of the Holy Spirit that teaches us to confess our sin so we can be healed (James 5:16)! I love the power of the Holy Spirit that makes us ache for God, so that we no longer find comfort in our sin, but instead are given eyes to see what binging and purging, or any of our pathetic, sinful addictions really are—enslavement (Galatians 5:1, John 8:31-32)! And I love the power of the Holy Spirit that teaches us to realize victory through him because through God's spirit we overcome again, and again…and even still again (Psalm 119:11)! Amazing!

I hate the thoughts and feelings of temptation. Makes me sick to know sin is creeping at my door (Genesis 4:7)—Yuk! But I love what God does when I allow him to take me through temptation victoriously! My friend, when I have endured temptation, I am astounded by the power of the Spirit of God in me that fought for him against my own strong will (1 John 4:4). Amazing! The struggle doesn't end. But I have grown strong against these struggles (Ephesians 6:10, 11, 16). Huge strength!

There are days when I consider my old habits, for whatever reason, and I do not blame Satan for everything that tempts me (James 1:13-14), although I know he would do a jig around me and my fridge if I gave in to binging. On those days, I cling to the help of God. Those days open my eyes to the reality I am nothing without Christ (1 Corinthians 10:12-13). That in all honesty is a beautiful day. Humbled, so humbled in those moments because who do I really think I am? You know? I'd like to think I am above temptation, but how prideful is that when even Jesus endured it (Hebrews 2:18)? I hate my pride! So, in those battle days (and, please, I pray you join me in this), I embrace the church that God has allowed me to be a part of (1 Peter 5:8,9).

I am blessed, so blessed, by godly women in my life that I know pray for me and that I know I can call in a heartbeat—that I know I have to be accountable to, and for purposes I really don't fully realize. But I use every power that God has put in my life to overcome the spiritual battle because he understands the weaponry that wins. Sometimes one weapon has a different tactical impact than another. Does that make sense? Some days it's God and me at war with his Word, and the battle is won quietly there. I read a verse, write it down, say it again and again out loud and in my heart, and in time the temptation dies. Some days it is the godly people in my life that help me overcome. I call a friend, tell her what I am going through, we pray together, and the temptation dies. I love God's church! And I know Satan hates that I love it, because he'd like to throw every doubtful and hurtful situation my way so I do not trust in the help of people I love, and who love me. You with me in that?

You ever wonder why there is so much conflict among believers? Women who love Jesus can let one another down! The body of Christ is a power source Satan is attacking constantly! We aren't commanded to trust people. We trust God. We are commanded to love people. I love the people of our church, and I trust God will work his purpose in my loving them, and their love over me. Hear me, okay? When I hid in my shame, I did not get better. It wasn't until I said my sin out loud—and not to God because he and I talked about it a lot! When I told another believer my struggle, I began to fight against it and claim victory. The Word of God is true! James 5:16!

Don't get discouraged because you are tempted. The Holy Spirit is in you, working on your ability to endure. Feed yourself the power source of God's Word for your mind and body. I will die in my flesh, even if it kills me (1 Peter 2:24)! I will die trying to discipline my body to live for God. I won't know the freedom of that release until I am dead, but I will fight, because in fighting I feel most alive in Christ. I refuse to feel the weight of that burdensome lifestyle again. I was lonely, depressed, unhealthy, and I hated what I had become. For my sin issues—for my flesh—I will always have to have accountability. I'm okay with that. I tell my friends who love me to ask me at any time how I am doing. And I also let them know when I am desperate for their prayers of faith to support me. Surround yourself with believers, my friend. There is power in the body of Christ.

God has not taken those temptations from me. I ask him to, but they remain. Ask him to take them from you. For some, he does. For others, not so. I'm good with it because I know God uses these struggles—and again I am not in a struggle all the time thankfully, but when I am, God uses the fight against temptation to keep me very mindful that I am dependent on him for all I am.

He keeps me close to him, humble, and merciful toward others who are in need of prayers and encouragement just like me!

One verse I hold to is "I can do all things through Christ who strengthens me" (Philippians 4:13). This isn't about like lifting cars or making a million dollars. This is about the sacrificial things I must do in order to live life for my God who loves me—whom I love. You claim it; memorize it, and call it out loud if you have to in the midst of the temptation. Food is an idol—the denial of it or in gorging ourselves on it—all empty rituals of idol worship. I pray daily to our provider God, "Give me this day—my daily bread." The bread that my body needs—not one bite more. The bread of life that is Christ…on him, let me feast!!!

I want to close by addressing your last concern:

Question: Will I always feel the need to "fill" myself with something?

Answer: Yes! You will. You were created in the image of God. You were meant to be satisfied by something; that something is him. He is your satisfaction. He is your completion. Go to him to be filled (Psalm 107)!

Listen to what Jesus said to the woman at the well who was looking for fulfillment, "Everyone who drinks this water will be thirsty again, but those who drink the water I give them will never thirst. Indeed the water I give them will become in them a spring of water welling up to eternal life" (John 4:13–14).

I get that. I know where my old water hole is. But girl, I am not going there. Because God changed the desires of my heart, I only long for what Jesus offers. Join me at the well of living water!

Love!
Laura

Selected Scripture:

Study method:

Truth learned:

Steps I will take to apply it:

My message concerning "Longing to Be Filled":

TRUE CONNECTION

D
EAR LAURA,
A man and women get married, and they obviously have sex. So the man (and woman) are opened up and their eyes, minds, and bodies are exposed to sexual things. Wouldn't it make sense for the man then to be more apt, anxious, and curious to be tempted with other things, for example, porn. For example, say a husband and wife have sex in the morning and then he goes to work...all day isn't he going to be all rowdy or anxious, thinking about the girls around him at work? Wouldn't he struggle more with his thought life and eyes? Does this make sense?

Reply:

Hey! Thanks for the question! I would love to answer this for you, but I really think we need the perspective of a godly man to help us think through your concern. So, if it's okay with you—and I'm trusting that it is 'cause you know I love you and want to help you as best I can—I've asked my brilliant, gorgeous, and most importantly godly husband to reply to you. Here is his response:

I can see how you may think this. Certainly there are men in the Bible who have fallen into this line of behavior. David and Solomon are two kings (and men of God by the way) who could not get enough of the physical encounters with their first wives, so they decided to get more wives. They eventually ended up with huge harems because of their lack of self-control...and this created some destructive situations and times for each of them.

One thing I think that these guys lacked—and other men of God who struggle with self-control when it comes to purity—was an understanding of the nature of connection. Let me explain. When God created man and woman, it was for one purpose—to connect with each other, with creation, and most importantly with God. But things went bad and now we are left with a messed up perspective of what true connection is. I think David and Solomon authentically wanted true connection in their lives. Read David's Psalms and Solomon's Ecclesiastes and you will see two men of God desperate for connection in their lives... for connection with God, with others, with creation, with their purpose, and with meaningful relationships.

This desperation is something we all have inside of us. Ecclesiastes 3:11 says that God has put eternity in our hearts. It is this "eternity"—this desire to connect with something bigger than us—something beyond us—a relationship that is true and real and forever—that we are inherently drawn towards. But at some point David and Solomon began to think that the physical act of sex was going to fulfill this need for connection. And they quickly realized that it did not quite meet the need and therefore they continued to try to meet that need with more and more women, without success.

So at the core of your question is the concept of true connection. In a marriage where there is real connection—connection to Christ first and foremost—and then a true connection between husband and wife...in this kind of marriage, the husband will have no need to explore other sexual options in whatever forms those take (porn, affairs, flirting, etc.). His desire for intimacy will be completely met by his wife because of their connection with Jesus and what he has made marriage to be.

So, sex between husband and wife should not fire the husband up to find connection elsewhere, but should fire him up to find even deeper connection with his wife. The true, deep, authentic, core intimacy found in this kind of marriage is one that cannot be duplicated or replaced by any other substitute. Satan will still try to convince the husband (and the wife in different ways) that their needs can be met outside of the marriage, but the attractiveness of these attempts will only pale in comparison to the true connection that can be found in a God-honoring marriage.

When my wife and I are deeply connected, I only become more apt to think about her, more anxious to see her again, and more curious to learn more and more about her. My drawing is only towards her, not towards other things. And that is the nature of God. When we truly connect with him, we are drawn to chase after more of him... more of the freedom in him... more of the purpose in him... more of the clarity of life in him... more of the romance that is our relationship with Christ.

Peace –
Kemper

And love!
Laura

Selected Scripture:

Study method:

Truth learned:

Steps I will take to apply it:

My message concerning "True Connection":

LETTERS BETWEEN MEN OF GOD

IT SHOULD COME as no surprise that guys think, talk, and act differently than women. This is what makes relationships so exciting, revealing, and challenging. In this collection, I get to share with you some insightful dialogues I have had with many guys in their college and young professional years. These conversations represent over a decade of ministry, but the issues they cover are timeless. And our creator God has spoken loudly about these issues in ways only he can, using wisdom only he possesses, and administering grace and truth that only he initiates. Most of us will deal with many of these issues, personally or through our relationships. May we lock arms and let God teach us how to learn, love, and lead well. I pray God's heart is revealed in every question, your purpose is clarified in every dialogue, and God's glory is revealed in every relationship you have.

Stay strong,
Kemper

CAN'T GET OVER HER

KEMPER,
I am struggling with the girl I like. I've been trying to love the Lord with all my heart, all my mind, all my soul, and all my strength. I've tried to do this by reading my Bible and praying regularly and I do my best to follow what God says, but I still have these feelings for this girl. It's gotten to the point where I told her she isn't my friend anymore and I can't talk to her. Basically I have to avoid my friends all the time at school because they're friends with her so I end up leaving any situation when she's around because they'll be with her and it just hurts to see her. She is a Christian and helped me early on by showing me things, but basically it's gotten to the point where I don't want to talk to her anymore. Yet I will still see her so I don't know how I'll ever get over her. It's just annoying because she's never had a boyfriend before and won't even date anyone and I feel like I'd marry the girl. I've never felt that strongly towards someone before and that's why it's so hard to lose those feelings. I pray so much that if it's God's will for us to not be together that he would make these feelings for her go away, but they don't. I get depressed about it all the time because I can't get her off my mind and she lives close to me next semester. Another huge reason I want her off my mind

is because I lust for her really bad sometimes and I ask for forgiveness after, but it ends up happening again. I don't want these feelings or attractions for her anymore because they've caused me to do wrong and I just want to please God without feeling like I'm blowing it every time I lust for her and give in. I just don't understand what I'm supposed to do if I pray for these terrible feelings of hurt and sin to go away. Sometimes I wonder if he's ever going to help because why would this still be going on if it's causing hurt and sin. My life has just come to be boring and lonely. I wish I could just meet someone that I could love forever and not have to go through this ever again.

Reply:

I'm going to try to bring some new perspectives to the battle here. Hopefully some of them will land with impact.

1. You mentioned that you wish that you could just meet someone that you could love forever. If you are a follower of Christ—if you have made him your leader, your life architect, your source of wisdom, your daily guide, and an ever-presence in your life—then you already have met someone that you can love forever. I think you are living where the church at Ephesus was living when Jesus called them out in Revelation:

    > I know your deeds, your hard work and your perseverance. I know that you cannot tolerate wicked people, that you have tested those who claim to be apostles but are not, and have found them false. You have persevered and have endured hardships for my name, and have not grown weary. Yet I hold this against you: You have forsaken the love you had at first. Consider how far you have fallen! Repent and do the things you did at first. If you do not repent, I will come to you and remove your lampstand from its place.
    >
    > Revelation 2:2-5

They, like you, were doing cool things for Jesus. They were helping people, they were working hard at their jobs, they got upset when they saw evil and injustice, they knew how to discern truth, and they had battled through some tough personal times. But, they had forgotten that they were in love with Jesus. They had started doing life with their affections focused in other places. They may have fallen in love with doing good, or knowing truth, or the attention that could have come from their public persecution. While these things are part of our lives as Christ followers, they should not replace our affection and connection with Jesus. And look at what Jesus says lies ahead of them if they don't re-align their affection...Jesus says that their effectiveness in their life ministries (e.g., at their jobs, with their families & friends) is about to be minimized—their lampstands are going to be removed. They are not representing the essence of the kingdom of God with their "good deeds". God wants our heart, and right now it sounds like your heart is turned somewhere else.

2. You are frustrated because God has not released you from these feelings toward her. What makes you think that God should do that? Did God turn off the feeling that Adam and Eve were having when they wanted to eat from the wrong tree? Did God grant Jesus' request for the cup to be passed from him in the garden before his crucifixion? I only shudder at the thought of what may have become of me, of you, and of all of humanity if God had released Jesus from his mission just because his humanness was having some difficulty grasping what was coming. God wants us to embrace the power he has given us to overcome our temptations and worldly drives. Paul compares salvation to a circumcision of the heart (Romans 2:29 and Phil. 3:3)—our core desire to sin has been cut away. But

as guys know (ouch), with circumcision there is always a piece of skin left. So, we have a piece of our fleshly heart still in us that we have to learn to overcome through self-control and discipline that comes from hanging out with Jesus and making his kingdom a reality in our lives.

3. You will need to get a God-perspective on this girl. If God has not opened the opportunity to court her, then you have to decide who you trust: your desires and what you think you want for your life... or God. Psalm 37:4 tells us to "Take delight in the Lord and he will give you the desires of your heart." I perhaps can hear you saying right now, "and I desire her, so it must be from the Lord." But don't skip the "delight in the Lord" part—it is critical. In fact, it is more than critical, it is essential. Delighting in the Lord, if I could put it another way is "falling in love with Christ" (see Rev. 2:2-5 previously), which is the consistent message of God all the way from Genesis to Revelation—he wants our delight, our affection and our attention. Once you focus your delight on Christ, then, and only then, will the desires of your heart come from God.

    As you have felt yourself, your desire for her is bringing you to a place of unproductive frustration, crippling lust, suffocating depression, and will eventually lead to vicious contempt... for her, for her friends, and perhaps for yourself. Do these qualities sound like those of a citizen of the kingdom of God?

    Focus on representing Jesus to her, protecting her purity (and her friends'), praying for her (by the way, that prayer needs to focus more on her growing closer to Jesus... not closer to you...let God do the connecting in your life). Remember, that your influence for the kingdom hangs in the balance here, as the influence of the church at Ephesus also hung in the eternal balance. Don't let some earthly desires and plans get in the way of the magnificent eternal.

4. We are called to freedom. Having to worry about not hanging out with some friends if she is around, adjusting your schedule and routes depending upon where she is, always feeling an urge to check where she is or who she is with—that is bondage...and a rough one at that. I have lived it and it was not fun in any way. I thank Jesus for freeing me from it... and he can free you as well.

Let me end with an illustration adapted from Prof. Dallas Willard: Let's say you wanted to go to Moe's to eat because that is what you really want. When you walk into Moe's it is affirmed that you are at Moe's with a hearty "Welcome to Moe's!" from the burrito crew (if you have not been there, you have to try it... at least walk in the door to get the welcome and then decide whether or not you want to stay). They don't say "Welcome to not Taco Bell!" They don't congratulate you on not going somewhere else. If you are at Moe's, by definition you are not at hundreds of other places you could be eating. But if your sole goal when you ventured out for some grub was to not be at Taco Bell, it is not really an effective way to get to Moe's. You could avoid Taco Bell by being at any number of locations, which are not Moe's.

So, what do burritos have to do with your situation?

Well you don't want to feel this desire for her anymore, right (the "not Taco Bell goal")? But, focusing on this goal is only going to make you think about her more and will bring loads of frustration...and really won't get you to your real goal of desiring God and his will (the "be at Moe's goal"). So, you need to focus on replacing your "not desire her" goal with a "desire God" goal. Then, you will get the "not desire her" goal thrown in as part of the deal. Let God transform you and reshape the desires of your heart. Just like when you focus on showing up at Moe's, it is pretty difficult to be at Taco Bell at the same time. When you focus on Jesus, it is going pretty difficult to be in a place of crippling, sinful desire at the same time.

There is no boredom or loneliness in God's kingdom. So head to his kingdom—Jesus is waiting to show you things beyond what you can even think of or ask through his power that resides in you (Ephesians 3:20). If this girl is not part of God's plan for you, then rest assured that he will have someone even better... way better...beyond what you can even think of or ask for. At the time, I thought my girlfriend in college was the end all for me. How limited my perspective was, and how incredibly grateful I am that God gave me my wife—she is beyond what I could have even asked for or imagined. Trust God. Trust his Word. Trust Jesus with everything you have and are going through.

Peace-
Kemper

Selected Scripture:

Study method:

Truth learned:

Steps I will take to apply it:

My message concerning "Can't Get Over Her":

DATING AN UNBELIEVER

KEMPER,
What does God say about Christian men dating non-Christian women? Should a Christian pursue a relationship with an unbeliever?

Reply:

Great question and one I wrestled with and rationalized about for a long time. Try some of these on...perhaps you are already wearing some of them:

"She doesn't know Christ... yet. That is why I am in her life."

"But, dude, she's hot!"

"If I break up, I will break her heart."

"If we break up, she will lose all spiritual influence in her life."

If who you are dating does not have Christ in her life, then she has another god in her life... and there is a good chance that it is called "attention". So, if the god in her life is attention, do you really think this will change when you get married? At some point your attention won't be enough anymore and she will look elsewhere. Remember that she has another god capturing her heart and it is not Christ.

While you all may have a great time together and connect well, you are fundamentally different at the core. You may share opinions on moral and ethical issues, but the foundations of these opinions are completely different. Her opinions are being shaped by the world and yours are being shaped by God's Word. At some point these will be opposed to each other. Her opinions can change quickly... and will. 2 Corinthians 6:14 says "Do not be yoked together with unbelievers. For what do righteousness and wickedness have in common? Or what fellowship can light have with darkness?" Light and darkness, no matter how hard they try or how much they want to cannot co-exist.

So why do some guys who seemingly are very close to God date girls who are farthest from God? This may be hard to understand...or is it? We, as men, were created to rescue, to pursue, to provide for. So, could some guys think that through their dating relationship they could actually rescue a girl from her sin? In other words, may we sometimes think that we can be her functional savior? Perhaps. But how crazy is that line of thinking? We can't change anyone, let alone save anyone. Let Jesus do what only he can do—don't act like you can be her savior.

And, consider the consequences of marrying a non-believer on what is the most difficult job in the world: raising kids. It is hard enough with a mom and dad who have the same faith foundation. Raising kids on two foundations—one of God and one of the world... now that is a recipe for trouble, frustration, disappointment, and destruction. Dad reads the Bible and gives the glory to Jesus while Mom reads People and gives the glory to the horoscope. Try that one on as a 6-year old who is struggling to figure out truth, trust, and life from mom and dad.

Need any more reasons not to date a non-believer? Hope not, but in case you do, here's one more. Let's say she actually does meet Jesus while you are dating her (but remember that this was not because of any power you had). Then she starts learning about what God's Word says about relationships and realizes that you were choosing to disobey God's Word by dating her. She then gets confused, perhaps angry, and maybe even pulls away from God given the hypocrisy in your life. At the minimum, she loses trust in your walk and character and that does not bode well for her view of God.

This was a great question—thanks. It is one that I wrestled with myself for years until a holy triangle choke hold helped me realize the truth of God's Word and the love that motivates it.

Peace –
Kemper

Selected Scripture:

Study method:

Truth learned:

Steps I will take to apply it:

My message concerning "Dating an Unbeliever":

FLIRT TO CONVERT

KEMPER,

What is the biblical position on 'flirt to convert'? There is this girl at work that is interested in me and she knows that I won't date someone that is not a Christian. She came to Bible study once and liked it, but I'm pretty sure she only did it for me. Should I keep inviting her, knowing that she likes me? Or should I just back off and let God prompt her heart to come?

Reply:

Recognize that including this young woman in a Bible study or church where she can hear God's Word spoken, sung, and lived out in front of her will never be a bad thing. Isaiah 55:11 says, "So is my word that goes out from my mouth: It will not return to me empty, but will accomplish what I desire and achieve the purpose for which I sent it." So, surrounding her with quality people, a cool environment, and a context of worshipping God is not going to be a bad deal.

However, your motives (or lack of romantic motive) need to be very clear to her. She needs to see the authenticity in your actions, character of your heart, and consistency of your words. Women will read into every little action and word from you, whether you have motive in them or not (this was valuable insight provided to me from Laura, my amazing wife, who knows the female mind waaaaay better than me!). So, if you ask her to come to the Bible study again, she may very easily read that you are romantically interested in her. However, you can innocently ask if she is coming back to the study, without asking her to come to the study. Did you catch the subtle difference there? To us guys, this difference may be immaterial. But to girls, it is everything. Just asking if she is coming to church demonstrates a lower level of romantic interest than asking her to actually come with you...but it still reflects your concern for her hearing and seeing truth.

So, don't drop the entire Bible study or joining you at church idea, but tread carefully. If she wants to come, but needs a ride, don't pick her up alone. Ask one of your female friends to pick her up, or take a female friend or two with you to pick her up.

Also, don't linger with her all night while you are at Bible study/church. Introduce her to some great Christian girls who you trust and who can hang out with her. Let her see what healthy Christian friendships look like. Don't feel like you need to be her support system and crutch. Make sure she clearly sees that your stance on dating non-Christians is a real heart commitment. She will completely respect that and if she is changed by Jesus, then she will dig your authentic commitment even more.

Peace –
Kemper

Selected Scripture:

Study method:

Truth learned:

Steps I will take to apply it:

My message concerning "Flirt to Convert":

DO NICE GUYS FINISH LAST?

KEMPER,

Why is it that women seem to be so romantically attracted to jerks while totally shunning nice guys? Why is it that the selfish man who treats women like "sex objects" manages to get the girl while the nice guy who treats a woman like a princess and would go out of his way and even give his own life for the girl strikes out left and right and is left lonely and single in the dating world? What do jerks have to offer to women that nice guys don't have that wins the hearts of women? Why is it so difficult for nice guys to attract women when the jerks seem to be able to charm women with little or no effort? This is a common issue I have noticed among women today, and as a nice guy who would go out of his way to make the girl of his dreams the happiest girl alive and treat her like a princess, I find this to be rather frustrating. It almost makes me wanna be a jerk, just so that I can meet women (which I would never do anyways because I am a... well... a nice guy).

Reply:

I will first share my perspective, and then will ask my wife Laura to chime in from a woman's perspective. Recognize that

Genesis 1:27 says that both men and women were made in the image of God, so I hope by seeing both perspectives, collectively they also represent God's perspective on this issue.

First, you are responsible for your own decisions and actions and not those of any girl or other guys involved. Don't settle for anything less than what Christ expects from you...and for your mate. Be a man of God that other men can imitate. In Phil. 3:17, Paul stresses to the church to continue to live to the high standards that they are being called to. There were (and still are) way too many people who claim Jesus with their lips, but deny him with their actions. Jesus distinguished these people when he asked, "Why do you call me Lord, Lord, but not do what I say?" (Luke 6:46). Be a model man of God for others to imitate.

Second, it sounds like your desire for a mate may be clouding some of your emotions here. Think about if your hunt for the right girl may be taking precedent over your hunt for God. When our hunt for other stuff in our lives pre-empts our focus on Christ, it can only result in some poor decisions and tough consequences. In Ecclesiastes 3:11 it says that eternity is in the hearts of men. We have an eternal longing, and when we try to fill that longing for something temporary, it works for a season, but never permanently. We really have only one model for our life—one longing that will never fail: the God-man Jesus Christ, who is the beautiful, wise, strong, and eternal one. Like Christ, our concern over the "bad boy" sagas that surround us should be about the souls, hearts, and lives at stake in the transactions.

Third, if there is a girl that you are interested in who keeps falling for the wrong guys, then she is probably not where she needs to be with Christ and therefore is not going to be good for you. You won't be the answer to her mis-aligned attractions. But Jesus will be. Check out what Paul said about the people he interacted with in Syria and Cilicia, "and they praised God because of me" (Galatians 1:24). Make sure this girl (or these girls) can glorify God because of what they see in you (your pursuit of things eternal and the integrity with which you treat people), what they hear from you (your honorable words of encouragement), what you think about them (your purity of thought), and what they learn from watching you (your knowledge of right and wrong and the resulting blessings of your obedience to Jesus).

Fourth, realize that the girl is never the big prize. God, through Paul's letters, constantly calls us to aim for the big prize, not for little prizes on earth. While an amazing wife is desirable and certainly a gift from God, as I can daily attest to (Proverbs 12:4, 18:22, 31:10), realize that our earthly marriages are only pictures of our ultimate and eternal marriage to Christ. Jesus is the big gift...the first prize. Don't get misled thinking that a wife, marriage, or girlfriend is the answer to your problems. She will never meet all your needs, and you will never meet all of hers. Don't let any woman take your focus off of Christ. Focus on running your race—Jesus has secured your finish, now you need to run it.

And lastly, to any "bad boy" reading this, I challenge you to consider your own actions in the context of what your maker designed you to be. These "bad boys" are the ones that claim Christ in their life, but treat women recklessly, with no honor, and as objects. These are the guys who talk about Jesus, sit in church, and run through the right "religious" banter, but then turn around and push impurity on women, encourage them to compromise for the sake of so-called "love", and ignore biblical principles about purity like they are above God's influence. These are boys who want to be men, but are too weak to act like real men. These are guys that lack the self-control, discipline, and strength that are character traits of followers of Christ. Yeah, you guys. I'm calling you out—you know who you are. Get real about what a true man is and does and says and thinks. Define yourself in Christ, not in your weak-minded sexual adventures and conquests. Define yourself the same way Solomon did after he realized the emptiness of his "bad boy" pursuits, "Now all has been heard; here is the conclusion of the matter: Fear God and keep his commandments, for this is the duty of every human being" (Ecclesiastes 12:13). For I also had to come to grips with the fact that it is only by submission to Christ that we find out who we are and what our lives are all about (see Ephesians 1:11).

Here is my beautiful wife Laura's valuable perspective:

I have to answer this question based on my own past attraction to the "bad boy" image. When I was lost—living apart from Christ—I lacked direction in every area of my life. When I realized who Jesus is as my Savior and Lord, his light went on in every dark corner of my heart and mind. The wild child boy was only attractive to me when I was not living in the awareness of my God and Savior. Once God opened my eyes to who he is, and how he loves me, my heart, my life, and my choices were all his. I tell you this to get to the core issue of your question. A girl who pursues a guy who is not pursuing God with all of his heart, soul, mind, and strength—who projects that "bad boy" image—is not pursuing God herself with all of her heart, soul, mind, and strength.

Paul is so crystal clear about this transition.

> So I tell you this, and insist on it in the Lord, that you must no longer live as the Gentiles do, in the futility of their thinking. They are darkened in their understanding and separated from the life of God because of the ignorance that is in them due to the hardening of their hearts. Having lost all sensitivity, they have given themselves over to sensuality so as to indulge in every kind of impurity, and they are full of greed. That, however, is not the way of life you learned when you heard about Christ and were taught in him in accordance with the truth that is in Jesus. You were taught, with regard to your former way of life, to put off your old self, which is being corrupted by its deceitful desires; to be made new in the attitude of your minds; and to put on the new self, created to be like God in true righteousness and holiness.
>
> Ephesians 4:17-24

174

The bad boy image that a guy projects through his sexy attire and attitude is an invitation that says, "come sin with me". That image screams without saying a word. Think about the advertising industry that uses sex to sell without spelling it out. We learn well from our culture how to sell the intentions of our heart, without saying a word. That dangerous image can even sit among us in the church sanctuary, pretending to be like us who love Christ, with us in worshipping him—in living for him—and without even making a sound, influence us away from Christ. And so that young woman, not yet surrendered to Christ—possibly wavering in her faith—or divided in it if she has found Christ at all, she is drawn to the allure of sin that she hopes will satisfy her ache for passion.

Don't be influenced. Stand firm. You see how easily it happens, right? All you have to do is open your eyes, look around at who is getting the relationships that you want and how they're going about it, and you wonder, if this is the image that gets the girl, is that what I need to be like? Don't be deceived. Keep your eyes on the image of Christ. That is truly the boldest, most attractive, bravest, most masculine image you could project. The image of Christ embedded on your heart and mind is the one that is required to go the distance in a marriage. It's a sacrifice, isn't it? To surrender what you see and what you want to what you believe through faith? You're becoming like Christ, my friend. "Follow God's example, therefore, as dearly loved children and walk in the way of love, just as Christ loved us and gave himself up for us as a fragrant offering and sacrifice to God" (Ephesians 5:1-2).

When I met my husband, we were both on a new journey in Christ. Kemper was a nice guy. I was totally drawn to him, and he did not fit the former description of my past "bad boy" boyfriends. However, as a nice guy, he had an edge about him that drew me. He was confident, never arrogant. He was secure in his faith, and he actively lived it out in front of me. He fought for purity in our relationship, even if the cost included me. He held on to his separate interests and did not allow himself to get swept up in me. He had a hunger for adventure, and one that didn't have to include my participation every moment, but sometimes would be shared with me as he told me stories about where he had been and what he had done. God was teaching Kemper how to discipline his mind and body, and he would not forsake those lessons for time with me. He did not let me become an idol. God was first in Kemper's life, and he invited me to share in that journey with him, as long as I, too, let God lead. That's hot! God knew it would be. Part of the curse in the Garden of Eden was that a woman would desire her husband—she would want to dominate him—but he would rule over her. With that curse from our loving, intentional, brilliant God, he also provided a cure, one that would draw us to himself: Submission. Check it out:

> Submit to one another out of reverence for Christ. Wives, submit yourselves to you own husbands as you do to the Lord, for the husband is the head of the wife as Christ is the head of the church, his body of which he is Savior. Now as the church submits to Christ, as also wives should submit to their husbands in everything. Husbands, love your wives, just as Christ loved the church and gave himself up for her to make her holy, cleansing her by the washing with water through the word and to present her to himself as a radiant church without stain or wrinkle or any other blemish, but holy and blameless.
>
> Ephesians 5:21-27

God's instruction is consistent, "sin is crouching at your door; it desires to have you, but you must rule over it" (Genesis 4:7b). Can you get the visual on that? Powerful. Dangerous. The most attractive strength you can project is your ability to master what desires to control you. Do not let your desires control you, and that, young sir, includes a woman. She is not sin, but her sin potential can master you. What she needs in her walk with Christ is to be able to respect you. Your strength to focus on Christ is everything. Check out Romans 6:12-14.

Focus on him, his image and no other for yourself, and for the woman who will one day be blessed by your understanding of his strength, sacrifice, and love.

Love!
Laura

And Peace –
Kemper

Selected Scripture:

Study method:

Truth learned:

Steps I will take to apply it:

My message concerning "Do Nice Guys Finish Last?":

NOT INTERESTED

KEMPER,
There is a girl interested in me, who recently became a Christian, and I am not into her in that way. How are some ways I can tell her that it ain't gonna happen?

Reply:

I am assuming that since you brought up the fact that she is now a follower of Jesus, that you can't use her not being a Christian as a reason to not date her. So, what you may want to say to her is that you are flattered that she is interested in you, but the connection that is necessary to move into a dating relationship is just not there. It would not be fair to her to pursue this relationship simply because she is interested in you. You both would be selling out and compromising what God has for you. She should be with someone who is all about her... and you should be with someone whom you are all about. Have you read the book of Ruth? Consider Boaz's selflessness and God-honoring actions that put Ruth under God's care. Boaz displayed the character and integrity of God in how he protected Ruth. Every woman should have a Boaz encounter when she meets you. You are capable of reflecting his character, as Boaz is a reflection of Christ. Even if you are not up to a relationship commitment as Boaz was, you can still do what is honorable. Rescue her from yourself with complete honesty. Of course, if this doesn't work, then you can always come with the "I look at you like my sister" line... that should do the trick.

Peace –
Kemper

Selected Scripture:

Study method:

Truth learned:

Steps I will take to apply it:

My message concerning "Not Interested":

THE THRILL OF THE CHASE

KEMPER,

I really need some advice and guidance about something in my life that has been burdening my heart for some time now. I have been praying and thinking about this a lot, but it's driving me crazy and I can't seem to stop my actions. For a while I was struggling with lust but, as a result of reading the Word, praying, and memorizing verses I have really learned to "bounce my eyes" from temptation. The thing that I have been struggling with though deals with the subject of chasing girls. I have been happily single for so long and always said that the girl of my dreams would just walk in on me one day. But recently it feels like a switch was turned on and I can't stop trying to seek as much attention from girls as I can. And it's not just a particular girl, or a few girls, it seems to be any girl I find attractive that crosses my path. I try to get their attention in any way I can even if it's just by a subtle smile, or simply a "hi." I have fallen into a trap of giving my phone number to all these girls and I hardly even know their names or if they are Christians or not.

The problem also comes when I acquire these numbers. It's not even that I want to pursue them, it's just the "thrill of the chase" as a friend of mine put it to me. I get them, we text back and forth, maybe a call or two, a trip to Starbucks and that's it. Then I try and break it off. I realize how big of a problem this is. I know that all girls are children of God but I am failing to live out this way of thinking. Why am I seeking all this attention from all these random girls? And most importantly why all of a sudden? I feel like I'm giving a bad impression to my Christian friends and coworkers when they see me do this day in and day out as I even do it at my job while I'm working. I clearly see the wrong in these actions, but I get so worried about what every girl who even walks past me thinks of me that I get overwhelmed! I need to put these actions to rest and give my full attention to God and his Son who doesn't care about what anyone thinks about me, only how I live for him. If you have any advice to help battle this, it would really help.

Reply:

Thanks for the question. I don't think this kind of situation is unique to you. In fact, I know it isn't, because I have talked to other guys about this kind of struggle.

Let's bottom line it, this behavior is not becoming of a Christ follower and certainly does not demonstrate Jesus to the guys watching you, or the girls you interact with. It may actually push them further away from Jesus. Let that one sink in for a bit...that you are pushing—actually shoving—people further away from Jesus with this addiction for attention. But to some extent, we all long for attention. The problem is we look in the wrong places for the attention. Psalm 16:4 speaks to our misplaced scavenger hunt, "Those who run after other gods will suffer more and more." The mental, emotional, and spiritual struggles you are having will only continue to increase as you run after another god in the form of attention from these girls.

The only attention that will ever be enough is that from Jesus. I'm not sure what you are looking for in these girls, but according to Ephesians 3:11, it is in Christ only that we find out who we are and what we are all about. You won't find your purpose, your hope, your meaning, your manhood, your confidence, or your esteem in these girls... or in the pursuit of these girls.

It sounds like your pursuit is part of your grand plan to find a girlfriend and eventual wife. Are those your plans or God's plans? God tells us to first commit our future to him and then our plans will succeed (see Proverbs 16:3). Are you committing your future to God? I know we can all say "yeah, sure, God's got my future" but do you really mean it? Because if you did, your behavior and decisions would reflect that. Your thrill would be in the chasing of God, not skirts. You would get way more jacked up when you hear from the Ruler and Creator of the universe compared to when you hear from any of these girls. Your contentment would come from living a disciplined life in the kingdom rather than collecting more phone numbers on your cell.

If you are having trouble figuring out how to get the right perspective about this in your life, take a look at Jesus' life—there are many places in the gospels where women were around him and part of the group of people following him (e.g., the woman with the alabaster jar in Matthew 26; Mary Magdalene, Salome, Mary, and Joanna among other women at the tomb in Mark 16 and Luke 24; Mary and Martha in Luke 10; the Samaritan woman in John 4; the women travelling with him in Luke 8) and you have to figure that there were many others who were clamoring for his attention. Study his mission—his purpose—his compassion and his spiritual eyes. He knew that the man side of his God-man existence was not the answer for any woman. But the God side of his existence was all the answer they needed.

Part of our existence on this side of eternity unfortunately is still in our flesh, as described in Romans 2:29. But we are also defined by our spiritual existence in Christ. Therefore, let your spiritual existence be what you portray to women. When God wants to bring the right woman into your life, your heart for God will be what they are most attracted to, I promise you. They will see a guy being defined and refined by Jesus in not only his words, but his actions, decisions, discipline, and how you honor women as opposed to playin' them.

This will take discipline...which at first may be quite difficult, but go after God and ask him to give you that discipline and to start seeing women how he sees them... and he will do it. He did it for me and still does, so I know he can do it with you and will.

One last point—note the truth of Matthew 6:21 (which speaks about where your treasure is there your heart will be also) that is on display here. Your treasure is wrapped up in the pursuit and therefore your heart is locked up there as well. By refocusing your attention, you will help restore your treasure in order to realign your heart.

Peace –
Kemper

Selected Scripture:

Study method:

Truth learned:

Steps I will take to apply it:

My message concerning "Thrill of the Chase":

READY TO DATE?

KEMPER,
What do you do when you are interested in someone but are afraid you might not be able to control your lust if you start seeing them?

Reply:

First, dating is not the enemy. Rather, dating is a place where we are to exercise our faith, demonstrate our purity, and develop the discipline to sacrificially love as God loves. It is also meant to be carried out surrounded by friends and family who can observe, support, encourage, and pray for you.

Second, we don't stand much chance to control our lust on our own—I am right there with you. So, I encourage you instead to consider if you are ready to discipline and control your bent towards lust using the power of Christ. This is the submissive stance we must embrace in our dating relationships (and marriage, by the way). If you are really "interested in someone" and that interest is pure and led of God, then you will do whatever it takes to protect her and her purity.

Of course, this does not mean that you cannot be attracted to her—that level of chemistry needs to be there. But there needs to be a mutual commitment to protecting each other's purity out of your love for Christ and to keeping the boundaries that you put into place together. If you do not feel like you can lead this relationship in purity—if your heart is not aligned with God's when it comes to things of purity—then you are not ready to be in a relationship. There is too much at stake when it comes to purity in a dating relationship at so many levels—physically, emotionally, mentally, and most importantly spiritually—to let your lust go out of control.

That being said, I am pumped that you are thinking preemptively about a relationship, knowing that temptation is coming. But submit yourself to God and resist the temptations that come and claim victory in Christ (James 4:7).

Fire in my fireplace at home is pretty awesome, as long as it stays in the fireplace. Fire outside of those boundaries would only mean destruction for my home. Dating and marriage can be incredible and amazing, if exercised within God's guidelines for relationships.

Peace-
Kemper

Selected Scripture:

Study method:

Truth learned:

Steps I will take to apply it:

My message concerning "Ready to Date?":

PEOPLE OR PROJECTS?

KEMPER,
I have this habit of coming across girls that are struggling someway in their life and I want to fix it. I end up getting them to tell me their life stories, and then I lead them to God's wonderful truths about salvation. The only problem I have is that after this I find it hard to let go. I almost become possessive to the point of wanting to know what they are doing all the time. I know this is wrong, but I don't know how to stop it. I feel that if I tell her all of this she will be crushed. Like at times I feel like I don't really care about them I just have to know what they are doing. I hate being this way and I think it stems from a heart issue I have about putting all my trust in Christ. I have accepted him as my Savior a little over a year ago, but I still struggle with giving everything over to him. I grew up with the idea that I was never good enough and that no matter what I did it was wrong. I would put my trust in people only to have it crushed or be used just to get something. Now I have become a doubtful person. I really want to trust God in all areas, but then I take that trust back. I also work in a very unchristian environment and there is lots of cheating and lying that goes on. I want so badly to change jobs but I have created a massive debt load and feel that if I quit I will be in trouble. I know I should trust the Lord to provide, but

I can't. I'm really scared to take the step of faith and trust him. Thanks for listening.

Reply:

Thanks for the question, it is a good one. You actually nailed the issue yourself in your second sentence. Check out what you said..."I want to fix it." Guys are fixers. Fixing stuff is what we love to do. The problem becomes when fixing stuff spills over into our relationships. People don't need fixing, they need Jesus. I can't tell you how many times my wife has come to me with an issue, and I have proceeded to immediately try to fix "it". The problem is that she never wanted me to fix it in the first place—she simply wanted me to hear her process the issue and to be there for her (the sad part is that this still happens... I am a slow learner). Part of our desire to want to fix stuff certainly has to do with our adventure-driven, pursuit-laden nature. However, we have to temper our desire to fix stuff with Christ's desire for us to be kingdom citizens with freedom to co-rule with him. Jesus didn't come to make sick people well—he came to make dead people alive. So, in a macro-holistic-eternal way, Jesus does "fix" people. But this is a complete overhaul of the soul, spirit, and desires of a person. It is a continual renovation towards the likeness of Christ. I almost hesitate using the term "fix" for what Jesus does, because our use of the term is so limiting and preconceived. The supernatural spiritual fixing was never meant to be our responsibility. But we are called to participate in the process by helping people run into Jesus in any way we can.

I was reading 1 Thessalonians recently, and I think Paul has some incredibly valuable things to say to us about our perspective on people. Let the weight and burden in Paul's heart for the people he is writing to sink in as you read this:

> Therefore, brothers and sisters, in all our distress and persecution we were encouraged about you because of your faith. For now we really live, since you are standing firm in the Lord. How can we thank God enough for you in

return for all the joy we have in the presence of our God because of you? Night and day we pray most earnestly that we may see you again and supply what is lacking in your faith. Now may our God and Father himself and our Lord Jesus clear the way for us to come to you. May the Lord make your love increase and overflow for each other and for everyone else, just as ours does for you.

1 Thessalonians 3:7-12

Despite Paul's tough circumstances, he found joy in their faith. He didn't take his own situation and desires too seriously. He found true life in the relationship with his friends in Thessalonica and with God. He never once mentions fixing their problems. A good friend once described it this way: do you view the people in your life as a project or as a person? If they are a project, then our focus will be on fixing them and making sure they stay fixed by keeping our focus on the diagnosis and solution of the problem. If they are a person, then our focus will be on their hearts, rejoicing with them when they rejoice and weeping with them when they weep (Romans 12:15). We will become less concerned about fixing their issues and more concerned about their hearts, their faith, and their relationship with Christ.

Paul's primary motivation is captured a little earlier in the same book in 1 Thessalonians 2:4 "We are not trying to please people but God, who tests our hearts." So you have to ask yourself, who do you really want to please? Others? Yourself? Or God?

If you want to please others, then you are telling God that his approval of you is not enough.

If you want to please yourself, then you are saying that you know better than God what you should have.

But if God is who we want to please, how do we do that? Hebrews 11:6 makes it clear, "without faith it is impossible to please God." Our faith in God's sovereignty in the midst of our circumstances, and in the eternal and unstoppable momentum of God's kingdom is how we can please God.

So, the advice I would have for you is to pray that God grows your faith (Romans 12:3). Get into the Word of God to develop your faith, as instructed in Romans 10:17, "faith comes from hearing the message, and the message is heard through the word about Christ." Read, study, and meditate on 1 Thessalonians about Paul's heart for the people in his life (note that this includes both guys and gals in his life).

Now let's move to the job issue part of your question. This is also a matter of faith...but let's first consider what may be typical advice you may hear regarding your job situation:

"I guess you have to either suck it up every day with these people or look around for another job and where there are lots of great Christians."

Or, maybe we can look at the situation from a more kingdom-centered perspective. Have you considered that it could be the sovereignty of God and his choice to put you in this job to be a light to these people? Have you considered that you may be the only representation of Jesus in their life and that you may be God's plan A for their lives? Most importantly, you need to seek out God in his revealed Word and let him talk to you about the fixing he wants to do. God may or may not fix your situation—regardless, he is much more interested in fixing you and your intimate understanding of his kingdom in and around you.

Lastly, I don't know of many jobs outside of working at a church or a Christian mission organization where you would be surrounded with lots of Christians. And even working at a church or a mission organization is full of challenges because the bottom line is that we all work at a place full of imperfect people with a bent towards sin. It is our responsibility to share the unwavering character, love, and hope of Jesus in what we say, think, and do with anyone and everyone we share life with, Christian or not.

Peace –
Kemper

Selected Scripture:

Study method:

Truth learned:

Steps I will take to apply it:

My message concerning "People or Projects?":

REALLY INTERESTED?

KEMPER,
There is a woman in my life that I am interested in. When we hang out together we flirt, and it seems reciprocated, but when I ask her to go for some one-on-one talking time, she always seems to come up with plans. Is this a relationship that I should pursue? I mean, does this seem like a "playing hard-to-get" thing or could it just be a flirt for convenience thing?

Reply:
It is hard to tell whether this is a "I'll play hard to get because I want you to have to pursue me" or a "you are a convenient and fun flirt, but nothing more" deal. Recognize that Scripture teaches a husband to honor his wife. Part of honoring her is pursuing her...as if she is an honored princess (which she is) that deserves pursuit.

So, the pursuit is an important aspect of any dating or marriage relationship. However, the pursuit of a girl who is only interested in your recreational pursuit when it is convenient for her is something to stay far away from.

What I would recommend is to put the ball in her court by letting her know that you are interested in grabbing lunch or some coffee with her and then asking her when she is available. If she is interested in you, then she will want to spend time with you. If she wants to spend time with you, then she will find some time to make it happen. If she still pulls away, even when you leave the timing completely up to her, then you will have your answer.

Matthew 5:37 says for our "no" to really mean "no" and our "yes" to really mean "yes". In other words, we are not to put on any sort of verbal facade. If her verbal "yeses" when you hang out consistently turn into "noes" when you ask for more time with her, it should be clear that her motives may only be the attention she wants when it is convenient for her... and then you can focus your attention elsewhere.

Peace –
Kemper

Selected Scripture:

Study method:

Truth learned:

Steps I will take to apply it:

My message concerning "Really Interested?":

NOT LOOKING BACK

KEMPER,
I have spoken to my girlfriend about this matter and we came to a decision that we need some guidance. We have been dating for almost a year now and before we came to Christ we were having struggles with sex. Until we really got into the Word of God and gave our lives to him (we gave our lives to Jesus a month after we started dating) we were still in this sin. Our entire relationship has been a huge struggle for me in terms of lust. I know what it is like to have sex with her because we had dated years ago also. As soon as we gave ourselves to Christ the thought of giving in to our temptations was out of the question for both of us. We gave up everything, even kissing after we were saved. However I still struggle with lust. Most recently I have been lusting over her like crazy. Just the other day is when the temptation got really intense, and we both gave in earlier today. I want to keep myself and her both pure. I also don't want to cause her to sin, and I know she feels the same way about me. We were doing so good. We both feel disgusted and hurt about our actions. We have known each other for a long time and have talked about limiting our dates to be only in public places and in groups. We both want to do what God would want us to do and

were just hurt and mad at ourselves that this could happen. Can you please help us out?

Reply:

You are in the middle of what I think is the toughest battle for men, and I am encouraged that you are fighting. Too many men who claim to know Christ are not willing to fight the fight we are called to fight. Get the point? It's about a fight. Some men think that saying a prayer at some point, or being involved in some ritualistic behavior (e.g., going to church, giving tithes, taking communion, getting baptized, having a Bible in their apartment) is all that Jesus could ever require of us. If that is so, then why does he talk about life transformation so much? Why does Paul talk extensively about fighting the fight laid out before us? It is because truly following Christ is about making him our friend, leader, teacher, confidant, resource, advisor, and daily savior.

It is too easy to rationalize sin—I know firsthand from the thousands of times I have done it. We lean towards thinking that Jesus could not possibly be asking us to withstand the temptation in front of us. We think there is no way that he could have ever imagined or experienced what we are experiencing right now. But we couldn't be further from the truth. Check out Hebrews 4:15 which says that Jesus was tempted in every way we have been tempted (and then some).

In Luke 4, Jesus was tempted by Satan to turn a stone into bread to feed himself—he was tempted to find satisfaction through his performance and abilities. Sound familiar in how we try to out-perform the next guy?

Then Satan offered Jesus control over vast cities and earthly kingdoms—he was tempted to find satisfaction in possessions and conquests. Sound familiar in how we try to have the latest and greatest materially and sexually?

Then Satan tried to convince Jesus to throw himself off the top of the temple in Jerusalem so that the angels could come save him and so that everyone could be amazed—he was tempted to find satisfaction in what others thought about him. Sound familiar in how we try to impress and live according to what others think of us?

Bottom line, Jesus is not some far-away religious figure who had some interesting things to say when he was on earth. He is desperate to be part of our lives in the here and now. When he prayed to his Father in Matthew 6:10, "your kingdom come, your will be done on earth as it is in heaven" does it sound like he was praying to a God who was to remain distant? He was asking for God's kingdom to become a reality in the lives of his followers now...not simply after they die. He wanted to reveal that God's kingdom was all around us. He wanted them to experience real and true life in Christ now. He wanted them to sense a part of heaven now... and the same goes for us. God's kingdom can be a reality now if we understand what the kingdom is and looks like.

So, what could it look like since 1 John 5:19 says that "the whole world is under the control of the evil one"? Ok, so how can God's kingdom be under the control of the evil one? This verse is speaking about the earthly system and how Satan influences many of the activities on earth (starting with the choice in the garden). So, there are parts of the world around us that are not characteristic of God's kingdom, but then many parts that are.

Consider these examples...

Humility is part of God's kingdom on earth (James 4:6), but false humility for the sake of attention is not. Compassion is part of God's kingdom on earth (Matthew 5:7), but compassion with a hidden personal agenda is not. Selflessness is part of God's kingdom on earth (1 Timothy 6:18), but emptying oneself for the sake of praise and adoration is not. Prayer is part of God's kingdom on earth (1 Thess. 5:17), but praying so that others can see our "spirituality" is not. There are a number of characteristics of God's kingdom that can easily get all skewed when our own agendas or pride gets in the way. The same goes for sex. Sex is part of God's kingdom (Genesis 9, Song of Songs), but sex outside of a marriage between a man and a woman is not.

I am wrecked for you and your girlfriend (and for so many others like you who may be reading this), that you recognize and pursue the things of the here and now kingdom, especially in the area of purity... and it sounds like you are doing just this. We will have stumbles along the way. But the key issue is how we get up and make sure that we don't trip over the same stinkin' fold in the carpet again. Smooth it out and be done with it—other folds in the carpet will pop up, but make sure this one doesn't.

Also, recognize that at this moment, Jesus wants you to run to him and him only. When my kids disobey me, I don't banish them to the basement—I want them right next to me so that they can hear my love for them and know that I am desperately trying to protect them. Are there consequences for their disobedience? Sure, but first and foremost, I want them to understand my love for them. So, let Jesus overwhelm you with acceptance and restoration. He wants you closer to him now more than ever.

We also have a tendency to dwell on our past mistakes and live in them to the point where we lose our effectiveness for future battles. If anyone had reason to dwell in past mistakes, it was Paul. But check out what he writes:

> Brothers and sisters, I do not consider myself yet to have taken hold of it. But one thing I do: Forgetting what is behind and straining toward what is ahead, I press on toward the goal to win the prize for which God has called me heavenward in Christ Jesus.
>
> Philippians 3:13-14

So when Paul says that there is one thing that he disciplines himself to do, I am listening. This one thing that he remembers to do is not to live in the past—he does not dwell on past battles... or victories. That is not what the kingdom of God is all about. Yes, we should remember how God has worked in us in the past, but we should not be positioned there. Face forward and be ready for the next battle...the next opportunity to worship Jesus... the next opportunity to show love to a stranger... the next opportunity to protect your purity... the next opportunity to take a stand in private that only you and God know about... the next opportunity to tell Jesus that you love him through your choices.

I encourage you with everything I have to be the protector of purity that we as men of God are called to be. It is so critical and so much hangs in the balance on this issue. 1 Corinthians 9:27 talks about the discipline we need to live with, 1 Corinthians 16:13 presents the man-strength we need to fight with, and Ephesians 5:3 speaks of the commitment to purity we must embrace. Make your life one of a disciplined fight for purity... and then you will experience heaven on earth—you will get to see the kingdom of God come in and through you. Feel the weight of Jesus' prayer to his Father personally—your kingdom come, your will be done on earth as it is in heaven—because it was meant for you.

Peace –
Kemper

Selected Scripture:

Study method:

Truth learned:

Steps I will take to apply it:

My message concerning "Not Looking Back":

PHYSICAL LEGALISM

KEMPER,
I feel, and have felt for some time that I want to wait until marriage for my first kiss. Even before I was a Christian I wasn't sure and of course not convicted, but now as a Christian it seems that I'm being more and more convicted. But to the world a kiss is something that people just do for fun. I never thought that this should be a flat-line rule for all Christians, just in my case. But lately I have heard many people talking and I was wondering if this is too strict of a conviction or if this is an acceptable boundary for me to have.

Reply:
First, this is a perfectly acceptable boundary to have, and one I would highly recommend. I love the testimony of Curtis Brown (formerly of the NHL's San Jose Sharks and Buffalo Sabres) and his wife Amy whose first kiss was at their wedding after the pastor pronounced them husband and wife. They both knew that even if they kissed while dating, it was going to evoke impure thoughts and put them in difficult and tempting situations. In my opinion, Curtis is a real man—a man after God's own heart— because he exercised his self-control and allowed his relation-

ship with Amy to grow emotionally, mentally, and spiritually in Christ. He protected her from himself and the temptations he knew would come if they went down the road of physical contact. Of course he was attracted to Amy—that chemistry is very important (check out the obvious chemistry between Solomon and his bride in Song of Songs). However, in Christ, he had the power to claim God's marriage gift and understood what boundaries it took for he and Amy to protect that gift.

Second, the world has a way of trying to remind us that what we stand for in Christ is weird, restricting, or just plain not right. The world had similar messages in ancient times too. I think this is why Peter, in a number of places in 2 Peter (see 2 Peter 1:12-13, 3:1) notes that he is "reminding" the followers of Christ what their life callings are all about. The world will never stop trying to remind us that we should just give into temptation and that sex before marriage is normal. What we need to do in response is to remind ourselves, by being in the Word of God, of what it means to be a follower of Christ. There is a reason why the Bible calls the true Christian life a "narrow road"—more people will listen to the world's reminders rather than God's reminders. So, let God, and not those around you, do the reminding in your life and let him guide your process towards purity.

Third, and most importantly, only employing a "boundary" strategy for our purity is a losing proposition. I tried a boundary-only approach before and merely extended my losing streak. Our core perspective on purity has to come from within us, not from boundaries outside of us. We must clearly understand the impact of sin on ourselves, those around us, and the body of Christ. This includes viewing sin as God does. Try this; think of the most disgusting thing you could ever eat. Now add a nice layer of warm, spoiled mayonnaise on top of it... and now sprinkle some day-old hair from a barber shop floor on top of it... and now picture eating it. Taste good? Your disgust is how we should view sin in our life. If we share God's heart towards sin in our life, boundaries have a much more effective influence on helping us remain pure. But if our sin is more attractive to us than our obedience to God is, then no boundary is going to work long-term. So, make your battle with purity a heart issue first, and then set up the proper boundaries, as God leads you, to protect your heart, eyes, mind, and relationships.

Peace –
Kemper

Selected Scripture:

Study method:

Truth learned:

Steps I will take to apply it:

My message concerning "Physical Legalism":

IN A MESS

K EMPER,
I've got some heavy stuff going on in my life. I'm addicted
to porn and masturbation. I'm going to just call it what it is
and be straight. I need some help in my life; I feel like I'm going
nowhere. I would call many years of near daily viewing or dirty
thoughts and masturbating an addiction. I feel a great sense of
purposelessness and no direction in my life. It's strange because
I am the example in my church, the guy all the younger guys
wanted to be like, and their moms wanted them to be like me too.
I am the guy all the girls' moms wanted their daughter to marry.
I'm the good guy, a missionary, caring, and my life shows that.
I've had girl trouble though: a nasty breakup a few years back
that I feel really backstabbed from. It seems like a black mark on
my life, and made me feel like I couldn't do a relationship. And
then recently I broke off my engagement with my fiancée because
I feel I am in no place to get married and have little heart to
fight for this girl and for my future—I feel desolate and hopeless
honestly. I don't know what I'm missing. I never dated or messed
around with girls outside of porn, but my fiancé and I toed the
line until it became grey and invisible. We're still virgins, but I
feel like I've let sexual sin just shoot down the best parts of my

life. I'm searching for truth, I'm looking for my heart and what I want to do in life, be it work, school, or continue in missions. But I don't have passion right now and I can't drag this girl around and let her hope for us when I don't know where I am going. I'm in a good paying job that has gotten old; I want to just get away and move across the country but I think I'll get into trouble with another girl, take her purity and be left with nothing but an experience and lost time.

I'm searching for direction. I feel kind of apathetic right now, because I used to have really strong morals against this kind of stuff. I need some accountability—I need to get this porn out of my life. Help.

Reply:

God has a lot to say about all of this stuff. It is heavy—heavy on you, but also heavy on God's heart too. He created you, and not for this stuff for sure. He created you for so much more and to glorify him in all you do.

First, I want you to consider these questions and really seek out honest answers. Not the answers I want to hear, or that you think God wants to hear. He knows your answers to these anyway, so there really is no use trying to deceive him.

1. Are you willing to do whatever it takes to get on track to becoming the man of God that he designed you to be? This is self-discipline.

2. Do you really, truly believe what God's Word says about the blessings of obedience and the consequences of disobedience? This is faith.

3. What are the major influencers in your life and what worldview do they have? Who or what are you listening to for direction and guidance in your life? This is where we search for wisdom.

Unless you can say with confidence "yes" to the first two questions, nothing I say here is going to matter. What you have described to me is a bunch of very bad outcomes. But outcomes can be traced back to your decisions, which can be traced back to the information you believe, which can be traced back to your objectives. Your objectives drive it all—they drive what information you seek, what you believe, what decisions you make and as a result, the outcomes in your life. If you are frustrated with the outcomes in your life, go all the way back to the source....your objectives, which are heart issues. The first question I posed deals with your objectives. Can you truly say that you want to do God's will? That you want to be obedient with your life and how you treat women and what information you allow into your eyes, ears, and head?

If you can with confidence before God answer "yes" to this question, then consider the second question. This speaks to what information you are allowing in your life and your decision making processes. If you truly believe what the Bible says about blessings of obedience and the consequences of disobedience, then your decisions will reflect that. You will start making decisions expecting the reward and avoiding the consequence. If you know the truth of God's Word, then engaging in sin just ain't stinkin' worth it. The consequences and risks are way too high.

The third question also speaks to what information you are allowing to influence your life and your decisions. Rather than yes or no, you have to do an inventory on your life influences and hold them up next to Scripture to see if they are steering you more towards God or further away from him. Paul instructs in 1 Thessalonians 5:21-22 to "test them all; hold on to what is good, reject whatever is harmful." Real men take responsibility for their obedience, for the women in their lives, and for the work they have to do. When you are allowing other influences to convince you otherwise, you are not taking the responsibility that God designed you with. By design, you are a leader of at least one person and if you want to lead others, you clearly need to know how to lead yourself. Part of leading yourself is knowing what sources of unhealthy information to cut off in your life.

Trying to live outside the principles of self-discipline, faith, and wisdom will only bring destruction. A fish may think that life would be so much better outside the confines of its bowl—that possibly a great adventure awaits. But as soon as it jumps out, it quickly realizes that this new and exciting freedom that it has will soon lead to its death. Within the fishbowl, it had complete freedom—outside the fishbowl, there was only destruction and death.

Joshua was faced with a similar situation as he led the nation of Israel into the Promised Land. This was a land that represented all that God had promised Israel—a place to flourish with their families and personally and corporately experience the majesty of God's creation. However, this excitement about their new adventure had to be balanced with obedience to God's commands. In Joshua 1:6-7 we find the Lord reminding Joshua to obey his law as he led the nation into the land and not to veer to the left or right. True success, true freedom, and true life comes from having boundaries. Within God's principles of obedience, we have freedom and true life.

As you have accurately identified, your lust and subsequent addiction to porn is at the root of much of the sin issues in your life. The other unfavorable outcomes in your life can be traced back to a heart's desire to engage in sin….which takes us back to Question #1. 1 John 3:9 says that no one born of God can continue in sin. Did you catch the truth here? If you are truly walking with Christ, you cannot keep habitually sinning. You simply can't keep intentionally choosing to sin, and I think you are realizing this principle in your own life. Sin wrecks you and then spills over into the lives of others around you and starts wrecking them too. Note that the verse doesn't say that those born of God won't start to sin—we all do. But the issue is do we stop our sin and repent?

Or do we let it go unchecked, free to destroy us from the inside out? You have to get to a place where you—all of you, your heart, mind, soul, and strength—are ready to be a man of God. Once you get there, then you can learn how to fight.

A friend of mine recently decided that it was time to fight his addiction to porn and masturbation. He knew it was wrong and it was impacting his life in major ways. At first, the fight didn't go so well—he was falling back into temptation easily and engaging in the sin he so desperately wanted to be free from. Temptation seemed to only increase. But my friend kept at it. He kept feeding his mind with truth. He kept sharing his victories and defeats with me. He was trying to live out James 5:16 which says, "Therefore confess your sins to each other and pray for each other so that you may be healed. The prayer of a righteous person is powerful and effective."

Soon, I started seeing a different fighter—one with more resolve, more experience in the fight, and more knowledge about how and when he was tempted to sin. One night he shared this with me, "I am truly learning how to fight." He thought that deciding to be a man of God was an instant thing. Adam was placed in the Garden as a complete man, but still had to learn how to fight like a man. We all have the ability to learn calculus, but we still have to work at learning it. You and I were made to be men of God, but we have to learn how to express that manhood. My friend had to learn how to fight like a man and is now winning. Through the strength of God's spirit, the truth is setting him free. I hear John 8:32 ringing true, "then you will know the truth, and the truth will make you free."

You won't be able to sacrifice for your girlfriend, finance, or wife and truly love them until you are able to conquer this sin. Lust, masturbation, and porn are all geared towards satisfying your love for yourself rather than your love for God. As a follower of Christ, your love for God must be greater than your love for yourself. You have to view sin as God views it—not as something that we can engage in with moderation or as long as we are by ourselves. Instead, we have to view it has heinous, as evil unleashed in our lives. Porn provides an outlet for selfish gratification—putting your desires before God. Your true identity is in putting Christ first in everything. When you understand that, then you can start loving the women in your life as you are meant to—by honoring them and protecting them with pure motives.

Bottom line, there are no good outcomes to porn and masturbation. Not one. It only stunts your growth as a man of God and the impact you can have for the kingdom. 2 Corinthians 10:5 instructs us to capture every thought and turn it over to God. The idea is pursuing a thief who broke into your house to steal everything you have, wrestling him to the ground, and dragging him to the authorities who then lock him up forever. Capture your thoughts, wrestle them into submission, and turn them over to God so that he can free you forever. I stand as a testimony to God's ability to free us from this addiction. After eight years of being controlled by it, I now have over a decade of freedom from the junk. He can free you too—stand up and take responsibility and enter the fight ring. I'll be your loudest fan and will have your back.

Peace –
Kemper

Selected Scripture:

Study method:

Truth learned:

Steps I will take to apply it:

My message concerning "In a Mess":

WHERE IS THE PHYSICAL LINE?

KEMPER,
How far is too far with a woman you are not married to? Where should I draw the line?

Reply:

Good question...but the wrong question. Song of Solomon 2:7 says to not awaken or arouse love until it is time. The eternal truth of this verse is that the physical nature of a relationship should not be awakened until marriage. This does not mean that you should not be attracted to your girlfriend—I hope you are. But you also are called to have the self-control to protect your purity, her purity, and your relationship.

And here is a line that I have heard many times: "but I luuuv her and this is how I need to express my love for her." You may have shared this line of thinking—I know I certainly did. My response to a line like that is to offer a challenge to study what real, true love is in the Scripture. A guy with this perspective may think that he loves her, but he doesn't in a rich, lasting, sacrificial way as God designed men to love their wives (or wives-to-be). If a guy truly loved his girlfriend, he would share God's perspective since God is love (1 John 4:8). God wants to protect his own, and purify them. So if you truly love her, you will do whatever it takes to protect her, her purity, and yours.

I wrestled with the "where's the line" game... and lost. Trying to figure out where to set the line is "sin management". God did not call us to manage our sin, but to conquer it. Don't lose this game—the consequences are brutal.

Peace -
Kemper

Selected Scripture:

Study method:

Truth learned:

Steps I will take to apply it:

My message concerning "Where Is the Physical Line?":

TRUE GRATIFICATION

KEMPER,
Lately I've been struggling with personal temptation. I've overcome the porn issue about a year ago by God's grace. He has eliminated all those images from my head. It's amazing. Lately though I've been struggling with the thoughts of personal gratification. I'm so sick of dealing with it! I've not given in, but I know what it physically feels like because of my past sin. Sometimes I have an extremely hard time saying no. I need practical ways of making this temptation much weaker or go away all together.

Reply:
You are recognizing the seriousness of sexual sin—it carries with it a powerful and lasting residual effect in our lives. I praise God for giving you the power to conquer pornography and pray for anyone else reading this who is in a place of dangerous addiction with the stuff. I've been there and through God's grace clawed my way out with his help, strength, and spirit. There is freedom in the conquering, but the effects of sexual sin can stick around. As a result, we continually have to make sure we are focused on staying pure and close to Jesus.

You are not alone with having a hard time saying no. Eve had a hard time saying no to Satan, Adam had a hard time saying no to Eve, and Paul had a hard time saying no to the things he knew were wrong (Romans 7). If this battle was easy, we could handle it ourselves. But we can't. That is why God gives us the tools necessary to fight. It is the hard battles that require both offensive and defensive weapons. Ephesians 6:10-18 gives us great insight into our weapons of war...and note the primary offensive weapon that has the power to kill: the sword of the Word. It is the Word of God that gives us power to destroy sin, withstand temptation, and cut to the heart of the issue. That is why it is critical to have the Word at your fingertips at all times.

I recognize that you can't always be carrying a Bible with you at all times...or can you? You can carry big chunks of it in your mind at all times and that is how you can attack these temptations you are facing. You can also have it within quick access from one of many apps on your phone. I love 1 Corinthians 16:13 which says (with my commentary in parentheses), "Be on your guard (temptation is always lurking and we need to be ready for it), stand firm in the faith (get grounded in Jesus), be courageous (act like the man God created you to be), be strong (use the man-strength God has already given you)". I am teaching this verse to my son, Kaden, because I think it is such a powerful verse for who we are as men and who we are called to be.

So, let's bottom line this with some practical ways to battle:

- Pray that God gives you clarity about sin and specifically lust, selfishness, and greed in your life. As Paul notes in Romans 12:2, we are transformed by a renewal of our minds. Where you place your thoughts shape who you become. Pray God aligns your motives, opinions, preferences, and thoughts with his.

- Get his Word in your head (Psalm 119:11). In addition to the verses earlier, 1 Corinthians 10:13, Jonah 2:8-9, and 1

John 4:4 (among many others) are great ones to have on deck in our minds.

- Avoid your temptation triggers: The places, times of the day, websites, and habits that all elicit temptation for us should not be part of our daily routines.

- Rejoice in your making: God didn't mess up with you. I have similar wiring with similar struggles. I praise God's design and recognize that he is glorified most in our self-control and obedience.

- Keep your eye on the prize: Do you think Eli Manning was thinking about anything other than winning the Super Bowl in 2008 as the Patriot defense surrounded him and seemingly had him down and the Giants defeated? Not a chance. He still, in the midst of incredible adversity, was thinking about how he could win the prize by getting the ball to David Tyree. Keep your eye on God's promise for purity in your life. I guarantee the truth of Proverbs 13:19, "the longing fulfilled is sweet to the soul", will never taste so good in your life if you stay focused.

- Get a brother you can trust: Find someone who you can talk to, who can ask you the hard questions, who can give you godly answers, and who can be the brother in Christ we all need. Proverbs 17:17 says, "A friend loves at all times and a brother is born for a time of adversity." War and pain seem to be bonding agents for men. Find a brother to fight this war with you—that is why we are here.

- Get ready for some pain, because in the pain there is victory. Continuing with the football analogies, no champion team gets to where they are without a preseason filled with painful workouts, grueling drills, and long days of suffering. But champion teams know that in the suffering of preseason comes the potential for victory. The truth of this principle carries weight far deeper than just the physical or mental. It is deeply spiritual as well. 1 Peter 4:1 says, "Therefore, since Christ suffered in his body, arm yourselves also with the same attitude, because those who have suffered in their bodies are done with sin." In our momentary suffering, we find lasting victory. When you say no to self-gratification, it may cause emotional, mental, and even physical pain…but the victory on the other side is freedom from sin. That victory is beyond any price tag.

Hope this helps.

Peace –
Kemper

Selected Scripture:

Study method:

Truth learned:

Steps I will take to apply it:

My message concerning "True Gratification":

WORTH THE FIGHT

KEMPER,

I have been dating my girlfriend for a few months. She is on fire for the Lord, we get along great and we have so much fun together. As a couple we have tried to make our purity a priority by not kissing each other or putting ourselves in blatant situations where we know we will be tempted. We are both very passionate people, which is how God created us. We have so much love for one another, and I am so thankful God has blessed me with such an amazing girlfriend.

Every day for me is a struggle. I have victory in Jesus, but Satan still tempts me. Satan tempts my girlfriend as well, both of us through thoughts and ideas. I have overcome pornography and physical gratification and my heart's desire is to be pure, but my flesh still wants what it wants. He who is in me is greater than he who is in this world, and I know I can conquer whatever Satan throws my way and I have. Sometimes it is such a battle for both of us to not kiss each other. It has not been easy, but it has brought us so much joy in knowing that it honors God, and I know God will help us stay pure. But if we are committed to being pure, why am I, and why is my girlfriend tempted to give into sin. We don't want it; I don't want it. The other day, she said that she doesn't know if she feels like she should be dating anyone right now, being tempted to sin and I don't know what to do or say in response. If we can't control ourselves now, who is to say we can control ourselves in the future, whether together or in different relationships?

Dating is hard; it really is. It is tough to love someone and want to express that love physically, but God has designed it otherwise, with our best interests in mind. I still struggle with temptation to think things. Is purity the absence of temptation or sinful thoughts and desires? Or, is purity the presence of those thoughts and temptations while rejecting to believe them or give in? I am not saying I embrace temptation; I hate it with a passion and I wish it were gone. But Satan is really manipulating the passion and love we have for each other.

Should we take a break and try and get things worked out before we try dating again? She is my best friend, and I do not want to lose her. She has helped me embrace who I am, who God has made me to be and is such a joy and encouragement to me and my family. I am trying so hard to trust God to do his will. I have surrendered this relationship to him, but why does this potential thought of not being with her cause my heart to break? I really feel like she and I have a great relationship because it is centered around Christ. So why is temptation coming so hard at us and how can we avoid it? We honor God in what we say and do, yet deep down Satan is pinching nerves and trying to attack us. Should I let her go and do her own thing for a while? Should I let myself go and do my own thing for some time?

I want to do what's right and I don't want to live in sin. My heart wants to fight for her; I don't want to give up on this relationship.

Reply:

Heavy stuff my friend. I hear your heart and I hope you hear mine... but more importantly, I hope you hear Jesus'.

Your struggle is one that we, as followers of Christ, have all faced. We face temptation, we wrestle with it, perhaps we even rationalize the resulting sin, and then we remember the truth of God and conquer the temptation and move on. But then we wonder what will happen next time it comes around? And how can I keep this up for days, weeks, months, years? Is this what Jesus meant when he said "let your will be done, on earth as it is in heaven" (Matthew 6:10b)? Surely, this can't be a touch of heaven!

This is where our faith gets its reps. Perhaps we aren't really getting what it means to experience a piece of heaven here on earth, to breathe holy oxygen, to sense the presence of the Creator.

Check out these verses:

"For my yoke is easy and my burden is light" (Matthew 11:30).

"In fact, this is love for God: to keep his commands. And his commands are not burdensome" (I John 5:3).

I don't know about you, but I have read these verses for years and am typically asking for a little help from God. How can following Christ be the narrow road (Matthew 7:14) and yet be "easy", "light", and "not burdensome"? Seems counter-intuitive and illogical, right? Understanding how these things are actually aligned and synonymous is one of the single most valuable things I think we, as followers of Jesus, can work towards grasping.

At this point, you may be thinking, "but when my girlfriend and I are sitting next to each other, you don't understand how stinkin' hard it is to not kiss her, to not have thoughts beyond kissing her, to keep my hands, head, and heart in check. It is as far from 'not burdensome' as I can get!" So, how can Jesus claim that at that moment in your life obeying him by choosing purity is easy?

Here it is: When you love Jesus with your heart, soul, mind, and strength, it becomes very hard not to obey Jesus. Too many people who claim to follow Christ settle for a life of trying to manage their sin while just holding on long enough to get to heaven. To some extent, they are missing the entire point of why God doesn't take us right to heaven once we are saved. Sin management is hard and will tear at a true follower of Christ. They will be torn at the core of who they are because you cannot serve the two masters of Jesus and your pride. At some point one has to take over and play the lead role.

When you get what it is to love with heart, soul, mind, and strength, you start to see the world differently—you start to understand the 'life of love' that we are called to (see 1 John for an incredible description of this kind of life). Because if you really love Jesus with everything you are, then you would love that girl sitting next to you with the love of Christ and would do anything you could to be Jesus to her...and for her. You would make it your mission to protect her purity, understanding that Jesus has given you the ability to do such a thing. Anything less would be hard.

And you know what? This process—living a life of love—is what I think Jesus is calling us to live. And it is that life that is meant to be easy, light, not burdensome, and a slice of heaven on earth.

Recently, I have personally been trying to really understand what living a "life of love" looks like—what it looks like in my marriage, in my parenting, in my walking through the hallways at the university where I work, in the times when I am by myself, when I am responding to emails, when I am in a restaurant... wherever, whenever. It is a difficult concept to try to grasp and implement, but I think when we do, we will truly recognize the easy yoke we are to wear.

A critical cog in our understanding is recognizing who Jesus really was and is as the God-man. Jesus wasn't just this superman who was pretending to be Clark Kent, acting like he could be tempted and pretending to be human. He fully embraced his humanness and suffered in major ways. He was tempted in every way we are. Yes, the internet was not around in the times of Jesus.

But, he was a young man who lived in a place where there were young women...enough said.

So, he can sympathize with us because he suffered and was tempted in major ways. When we are weak, we need to run to Jesus, not from him in shame. When we are tempted, he is not disappointed. Rather, he sympathizes with us. He wants to embrace you as a father, friend, and brother. The writer of Hebrews captures this in Hebrews 4:15, "For we do not have a high priest who is unable to empathize with our weaknesses, but we have one who has been tempted in every way, just as we are—yet he did not sin."

Temptation will continue. Resist it, and say yes to God because saying yes to temptation is saying no to God. When you live a life of love, saying yes to God becomes just part of who you are. When we run to Jesus, the writer of Hebrews tells us what we are guaranteed to receive, "Let us then approach God's throne of grace with confidence, so that we may receive mercy and find grace to help us in our time of need" (Hebrews 4:16).

So, recognize that your temptation is not the sin. Scripture makes that clear when it says that Jesus was tempted, but was still without sin. It is your response to temptation that you are wrestling with. Fight for your relationship with your girlfriend. It sounds like both of you are committed to Christ first and foremost which is the key. Keep focused on him and embrace, practice, and engage in a life of love.

There are certainly things you can do to minimize the opportunities for temptation. But trying to eliminate temptation completely is not something that you should be focusing all your energy on. How to respond to it when it comes—now that is where you should focus most of your energy. And when this response becomes 'easy' then you will have more energy to worship Jesus with all you do each day. Satan's tactics are designed to convince you that giving into the temptation will be worth it and will be much more fulfilling than obeying God. But it just ain't. Remind Satan that he is nothing but a sorry liar and then give him some truth from God's Word to choke on, and then thank God for being who he is.

I pray following Christ for all of us can become simply who we are, what we are all about, second nature to us, and something that is...easy.

Peace –
Kemper

Selected Scripture:

Study method:

Truth learned:

Steps I will take to apply it:

My message concerning "Worth the Fight":

CONFRONTING A BROTHER

IN THIS ENTRY, there are two related questions that I am combining as they deal with similar issues.

Kemper,
How do you confront a brother who is in sexual sin?

Kemper -
I have a situation I could use some wisdom and advice on. First, let me preface by saying I need to pray more about this. I've recently moved in with three Christian guys from school. Over the past few weeks, I've been noticing my one friend who is in a relationship has been falling asleep on the living room couch with his Christian girlfriend. His girlfriend lives about 15 minutes away with some other Christian girls on campus. This happens multiple times each week and often she gets up very early to leave before the rest of us get up for work. I have also "surprised" them on accident in the midst of something physical. I've not discussed this with my other two roommates.

My friend and his girlfriend may have set their own boundaries and may not be tempted where they are. But I feel their laying together on the couch at night watching TV and falling asleep together presents the wrong kind of image. The way she leaves seems secretive too. I wonder what her roommates think she does when she sleeps over. Maybe they are totally okay with it, but my opinion is that they're on the edge of the cliff. Should I bring it up with them? If I'm just critical, judgmental, or wrong, I'd rather not stir the pot. But if there is something my friends need to hear from God to prevent them from creating a bad image/falling into sin, should I be the one to speak to him as a brother in Christ? If so, where would I look to for words of grace and love that wouldn't offend? Thanks for your insight/experience.

Reply:

A typical answer that you may get from someone about this particular issue may go something like this:

"The clear thing to do is to ignore the issue. Our lives are private, and you should just mind your own business. Give your roommate the privacy that he and his girlfriend so clearly deserve. In fact, you may want to think about encouraging them to seek more privacy in his room."

The problem is that God did not call us to be typical. In Jesus' prayer as recorded by John, he says:

> I have given them your word and the world has hated them, for they are not of the world any more than I am of the world. My prayer is not that you take them out of the world but that you protect them from the evil one. They are not of the world, even as I am not of it. Sanctify them by the truth; your word is truth.
>
> John 17:14-17

Let that sink in a bit and realize how atypical we are called to be. So, with that backdrop, let's dive in.

There is a part in all of us guys that like a good fight—something to rescue, a truth to fight for, a conquest to pursue. Both John Eldridge in *Wild at Heart* and Erwin McManus in *The Barbarian Way* discuss this God-given fiery side in us. However, for some reason when it comes to confronting a brother—a friend—a roommate—that becomes tougher. Many of us don't want to lose a friend and we realize that a confrontation may result in just that. So we avoid any kind of conversation about sexual purity. But when we know the right thing to do and choose not to do it, that is also sin (James 4:17).

Fortunately, God's Word has plenty to say about how we can do this effectively. Realize that we can go about it the same way that Jesus approached the world, including his friends….with humility, love, grace, and truth. Paul captures this in his letter to Ephesus:

> Instead, speaking the truth in love, we will in all things grow up into him who is the head, that is, Christ. From him the whole body, joined and held together by every supporting ligament, grows and builds itself up in love, as each part does its work.
>
> Ephesians 4:15-16

So, we are to speak the truth in love and by doing this it helps us not only grow up as men, but helps the entire body to grow. Confronting with a prideful agenda and arrogant mindset will only be unproductive. Be real, be honest about your own struggles, and be authentic with him.

Privacy and 'horizontalness' are both not only dangerous, but are not part of biblical instruction about our relationships with women and with our friends. It sounds like you have processed this issue and have landed in a good spot. You have nailed some of the most dangerous issues about this scenario. I'll try to help with some further validation and strategies for talking to your roommate.

Scripture has a lot to say about privacy. While privacy with God is critical to develop our spiritual disciplines (e.g., dedicated time in the Word, meditation, Scripture memorization, fasting), personal privacy—time where we do what only we want to do—

is not critical to our development. Personal privacy is telling God that there are parts of your life that you don't want anyone else prying into, including God. If God is all-powerful, all-knowing, and all-good, how ridiculous is this way of thinking anyway?

So, while your roommate and his girlfriend may be disciplined within their boundaries (which, by the way, I doubt their discipline will remain strong given the temptations they are exposing themselves too), there are a number of other issues at hand that you can address. Check out Ephesians 5:3, "But among you there must not be even a hint of sexual immorality, or of any kind of impurity, or of greed, because these are improper for the Lord's people." As you so accurately note, they are setting a dangerous example for others around them including you, your roommates, your friends, the girlfriend's roommates, and their friends. There are all kinds of "hints" of immorality going on here. Being horizontal is hint enough. Add in some all-night longevity and some early morning escapes, and we have some full on hints, clues, and suggestions.

Notice what Paul tags onto the end of his statement about sexual immorality and impurity—he says "or of greed". So, where does immorality and impurity come from? How about greed? How about wanting something for ourselves that we think we deserve or want, or something that someone else has? Your roommate and his girlfriend have probably rationalized that this is something that they deserve to do, they like doing it and besides, they are not having sex, right? Remember, sex is a process, just like having a baby is a process. Are they engaged in part of the sexual process? Absolutely. Can they disengage their lustful thoughts and images while in the throngs of this process? I would sincerely doubt it. I can bet their minds are racing with the thoughts of what comes next...and what comes next will indeed come if they let their hearts go unguarded here. Bottom line, we don't need to be getting horizontal with a girlfriend—there is really nothing good that could ever come out of it. Your roommate needs to consider what Jesus says about the stumbling blocks that we create for our brothers in Luke 17:1-3.

If left un-checked, you and your roommates may look back on this one day and rationalize your own 'horizontal' privacy, thinking that "since he did it, it must be ok." Also, who knows what her roommates are thinking. For girls, this may be even a more dangerous precedent, but I sure hope her roommates are also praying about talking to her and searching for the wisdom and grace to do so.

What you and/or your other roommates may want to think about doing is setting up some kind of house accountability that encourages you all to become the men of God that we are called to in 2 Timothy 1:7, "For the Spirit God gave us does not make us timid, but gives us power, love and self-discipline." Paul is talking to his main man, his confidant, his brother in Christ, Timothy, making it clear what a man of God is called to. By talking to your roommate, you will be helping him truly love his girlfriend with power and self-control, in ways he is called to, by honoring and protecting her. In 1 Corinthians 16:13, we get another glimpse of what authentic manhood looks like, "Be on your guard; stand firm in the faith; be courageous; be strong." Your roommate's "alert" monitors seem to have been disabled, so you need to stand firm in the faith to help him be courageous and strong. Here are some ideas that may help protect all of you, while drawing you closer to Christ.

- Ask him what you and your other roommates can do to help the situation. He may know that he is living a dangerous and comprising life in this area, but may not know how to get out of it. Help from you guys may save his life.

- You and your roommates could start a Bible study or devotional on purity.

- Set up some house expectations that you and your room-mates agree to and hold each other accountable for. Here are some suggestions: No girls in the apartment after midnight. No co-horizontal action. No topic is off limits to talk to each other about. Equal time with the remote. Equal time on the dishes. The last two are slightly off topic, but still help build an environment of trust and equity.

Also, he doesn't have to be your best friend to have a conversation with him. If I saw any friend of mine walking slowly towards a cliff, but he was having a great time as he was walking—laughing, enjoying life, but not considering the consequences of his actions and what lies ahead of him, I would certainly be trying to get to him as quick as possible to let him know what he was about to step off into. And as for what I would say when I got to him? I'd trust God to give that to me. In Luke 21:15, Jesus assures us that he will give us the words and wisdom we need when we step out in courage.

More generally, here is a framework to consider when confronting a brother about any habitual, intentional sin.

1. Make sure he is really a Christian. His sin may be because he does not know Christ. Going to church does not make you a Christian just like showing up on a college campus does not make you a student there. Saying that you are a Christian does not make you a Christian either. Christ said that you will know his followers by their obedience and the fruit in their lives. So, first and foremost find out where he is with Jesus. If he does not know Christ, then you need to focus on sharing the eternal truth and present hope of Jesus with him.

2. If he knows Christ, then his deepest desire will be to obey God and you can share with him truth about obeying God, especially in the area of purity. Share with him the truth of lust in Matthew 5:28, or fornication in 1 Corinthians 6, or another scripture on purity. Ask him if he is willing to do whatever it takes to get out of his sin. If he is, then ask how you can help him, being authentic about your own struggles as well. Accountability is huge, prayer is enormous—be there for him any way you can.

3. If he does not respond then you may have to bring in other godly friends—perhaps your roommates, as outlined in Matthew 18. Together you can collectively express your concern and love for the dude and explain that you all are not going to give up on him. Be the brothers described in Prov. 17:17 who are born for adversity.

4. If he still does not respond, then you approach leadership at your church or ministry you are part of. Talk to some pastoral leaders about approaching your friend in love and truth.

5. If this still does not work, then you have to let him proceed while being ready to love him at any moment. Remember the prodigal son? The father let the son go do what he wanted to do, and I bet the father had tried everything he could think of before that. As tough as letting him do what he wants to do may be, you can't make decisions for him and he has to live out the consequences of a disobedient life on his own. But be ready to love him when he returns, as the father was when his son returned. Celebrate his return and choice of obedience, and continue to pray for him in the meantime.

Peace -
Kemper

Selected Scripture:

Study method:

Truth learned:

Steps I will take to apply it:

My message concerning "Confronting a Brother":

FEMALE BEHAVIOR

KEMPER,
I have a question about physical intimacy between Christian females. I'm not sure if this is something common with Christian girls or what, but it concerns me. I'm referring to cuddling, touching, long hugs, etc. It doesn't appear very sexual, but if I was dating a girl and she did any one of these things with a guy it would definitely be regarded as cheating. Is it different if she does it with a girl? Some people have commented that if they didn't know the girls, they would have thought that they were lesbians.

So how physically intimate can two females be before it is considered sinful? And, how should I address this if a believer that I know is engaged in this? My concern is that if a girl is getting emotional and physical attention from a female, can a boyfriend even compare? I don't ever want to be in competition with another female for my girlfriend.

Reply:
You are not alone in your observations as I have heard this from other guys who are concerned as well. Bottom line, it is a behavior that is not wise. As always, we have to filter the issues of our life through what God's Word says. While I can't show you a

verse that addresses two female believers engaged in public cuddling and touching, there is plenty of teaching about whether this is wise and behavior characteristic of a follower of Christ (by the way, I can't show you a verse that says not to eat a muffler either, but clearly it is not wise).

First, sin always starts somewhere. This kind of behavior may not be sin, but it certainly could create an atmosphere that is conducive to sin. David's stroll around his roof in 2 Samuel 11 was not sin, but it put him in an atmosphere that led to a number of sinful choices. In Proverbs 4:14, Solomon instructs his son, under God's leading, to not enter the path of the wicked and not to proceed in the way of evil men. But notice that he does not say, "do not become wicked or evil." Rather, he instructs us to not even enter the path—not to enter into the way of those that make wicked decisions—not to find ourselves in situations that could lead to sin. We need to fight for purity in our earthly relationships in order to glorify our relationship with our Creator.

Second, is it the wise thing to do? Proverbs gives us great instruction in the way of wisdom (Proverbs 4:11). We always have to ask, "Is this the wise thing for me to do given my past experiences, current circumstances, and future plans?" (see Andy Stanley's book, *The Best Question Ever*). I have tried and I can't envision a set of experiences, circumstances, and plans that would promote this practice as wise.

Third, does it cause someone else to stumble? Perhaps their motives are pure, but as Paul notes in 1 Corinthians 8:13, he will not engage in activities that may cause another to stumble (his example was food, but the underlying timeless principle is clear). This kind of behavior not only may cause the girls involved to stumble, but it may cause the guys observing it to stumble in their thoughts. Guys can easily pervert the scene in their mind which does not lead to a healthy place mentally. Jesus gives us a strong warning about causing others to stumble in Luke 17:1-2. These girls need to know that this kind of behavior could certainly cause others, of both genders, to stumble.

Fourth, does it glorify God? 1 Corinthians 10:31 teaches us to glorify God in all we do—not just when we sit in church or get the promotion at work we really wanted or get accepted into the college we hoped to attend or when that girl you have noticed for months finally notices you. It is easy to glorify God in this stuff. But we are to glorify him in the hard stuff too including keeping our thoughts and motives pure around people, not coveting the stuff of the world, not giving in on small things that no one except God would ever know, and protecting our relationships from impurities. These are the hard things that we have to be disciplined in to glorify God.

Lastly, as you have wisely noted, if the girls are getting the attention they need from another girl, they are setting a dangerous precedent and may learn not to expect it from a guy—this works against God's creation. God created man and woman to become one in marriage (Genesis 2:24)—mentally, emotionally, physically, and spiritually. If the physical and emotional needs are fulfilled by a girlfriend, their marriage will never be what God designed it to be.

So, where do you go from here? Consider the instruction of Proverbs 27:5-6 which says that an open correction is better than love that is concealed. True love shares truth and any temporary wounds that come from a friend are faithful. Overlooking opportunities to share truth in love is deceitful and, in effect, becomes the enemy of your friend. So pray for wisdom in your words (James 3:17)—wisdom that represents purity, promotes peace, is gentle in spirit, reasonable and rational, and full of mercy, grace, love, and truth. Also pray for the right time to talk to her. Proverbs 25:11 talks about how truth spoken in the right circumstances (including at the right time) is beautiful. God will give you an opportunity—be real, be honest, be humble…be like Jesus.

Peace-
Kemper

Selected Scripture:

Study method:

Truth learned:

Steps I will take to apply it:

My message concerning "Female Behavior":

FOCUS OF OUR AFFECTION

KEMPER,
What could you say to encourage myself and those who have lost a desire for God, but still know deep down they truly do want a passionate relationship with him?

Reply:
You are not alone in this longing. In fact, I would guess that this issue has surfaced for just about every follower of Christ at some point in their relationship with him. For many, the loss of desire for God starts small. We are enticed by small things that we think won't really damage us. These small enticements then slowly (or rapidly for some people) grow to the point where we have lost sight of God—where we have lost our passion for him—where we are somewhere we do not want to be and can't really even figure out how we got there. We start making small choices that we know are not consistent with what God wants for us. We start to make compromises in critical parts of our lives (purity, relationships, discipline). We start being enticed by the lies of the evil one and running after other gods (Psalm 16:4a).

Peter talks about this "enticement" in 2 Peter 2:18 (and it shows up in James 1:14 also) and the connotation of the word "enticement" in the original text is one of enticing fish with some bait so that they can be snared with a sharp hook. It is the apparent promise of satisfaction, gratification, and/or freedom that only leads to our capture, pain, and destruction. For men, this enticement many times comes in the form of lust, fornication, adultery, materialism, addiction, pride, and/or anger. Then when the temptation to give into these sins hits us... and it will... we tend to think that forsaking obedience to God on any of these items will be worth it. But no one makes this exchange and in the long run is thankful for it. And don't think you are going to be the first. Sure, short term, it may feel rewarding...but feelings are fleeting and the consequences will soon greatly outweigh any perceived "reward". And "greatly outweigh" is an understatement; it is more like infinitely outweigh.

In Jeremiah 2:1-3, the Lord is speaking and is talking to his people (the nation of Israel at the time, but the principles apply to his church today). He is recalling a time when they were fired up and passionate for him. The Lord blessed them and protected them from their enemies. But, as captured in Jeremiah 2:11, they started being enticed by worthless idols. They started viewing their sin as more attractive than God. Note the significance of Jeremiah 2:12 when the angels in heaven are appalled at this behavior from God's people. Why are they so appalled? Because they know the awesomeness of God—they know how flippin' amazing it is to worship God, and they are freaking out because his people are acting like their obedience to God is priority #5... or #10... or #1,638... or anything but #1 in their lives.

The same goes for us today. If we truly understood the grace and love we have been shown as adopted kids in God's kingdom, any temporary rewards from our choices to sin would just not be worth it... period. Whatever is enticing you today, tomorrow, next week, or right now... God is better.

So, what do you or I do in this situation? First, realize that there is no recipe to loving God. There are no 12-step recovery programs. We live in a microwave generation where we want results fast, easy, and repeatedly. As Christians, we have to unlock our hearts and let our new nature in Christ out. If you are truly a follower of Christ, then your deepest desire will be to follow him and to obey him. You have to let this deepest desire rule your life and be your sole focus.

But what if you simply don't feel the joy of following Jesus? Then you have to man-up and choose joy. Lead with your obedience and your feelings will follow. Feelings make awful leaders, but great followers. Do you think Jesus felt completely joyful as he approached the cross? But Hebrews 12:2 says, "For the joy set before him he endured the cross." Jesus endured the cross because he understood that the hope, reconciliation, and salvation of the world hinged on the cross. Obedience preceded joy.

You have to focus on renewing your passion for God through heart, head, soul, and strength. Recognize the presence and hope of Christ every moment of every day of your life and then choose to live life with him... really live life with him and for him.

1 Thessalonians 1:9 says, "for they themselves report what happened when we visited you. They tell how you turned to God from idols to serve the living and true God."

Turn and serve—that is about as close to a recipe as you are going to find. But make it personal... because God is personal.

I pray you are never the same again as you encounter the true God in ways you never imagined. He will provide all the enticement you will ever need.

Peace –
Kemper

Selected Scripture:

Study method:

Truth learned:

Steps I will take to apply it:

My message concerning "Focus of Our Affection":

LEADERSHIP DEVELOPMENT

KEMPER,
As a newer Christian, I am so fired up for the Lord and I just feel like I need to tell everyone! But some people where I work always try to put me down, and it gets so frustrating. I just don't know how to respond to them without getting upset. I am into the Word every day because as it says, "study to show yourself approved" (2 Timothy 2:15a). I want to be the best witness possible so I can truly tell these people what the Lord has done for me, and what he can do for them also. I'm not trying to change them or anything. I would just like to let them know that I am a follower of Jesus Christ, and that I am very proud of that. I need some help so I won't get upset when these people put me down, or tell me how what I believe is not true. I just don't know what to say, and I kind of just blank out and end up walking away frustrated and questioning my own faith. If you have any insight, it would be greatly appreciated!

Reply:
The title of this section and the question may seem disconnected—what does getting put down at work have to do with leadership? But there are some key issues in leadership develop-

ment that are surfacing here. Recognize that by expressing your faith in meaningful ways that display the kingdom of God in your life, your development as a leader is being cultivated and trained. When you get married, you are expected to be the spiritual leader—the temperature setter of the home. You will have to stand up for your household, as Joshua did in Joshua 24:15b when he said, "as for me and my household, we will serve the Lord." You will be expected to stand up for your faith, for your family, for your kids, for what is right, for principle over popularity, for character over compromise, for self-control over self-indulgence. So, the stand you are taking and the example you are living is laying the foundation for your future relationships. So, how do you navigate this apparent landmine of opinions, ridicule, and frustration?

First, have confidence in who you are in Christ, because Jesus says in Luke 12:11-12, "When you are brought before synagogues, rulers and authorities, do not worry about how you will defend yourselves or what you will say, for the Holy Spirit will teach you at that time what you should say."

This doesn't mean you have to be standing before rulers. The passage rather implies that when you are hanging out with people who think they know more than you and have convincing sounding arguments, don't worry because the wisdom that comes from God is unmatched. God will give you the right words to say to your co-workers at the right time.

Second, be careful not to be the guy who judges and proclaims hell for everyone around him. Be the person we are called to be in 1 Peter 3:15, "Always be prepared to give an answer to everyone who asks you to give the reason for the hope that you have. But do this with gentleness and respect." Be merciful and full of grace, because that is how Jesus is with you. Be real and honest about your mess-ups and what God has done for you and with you. Share your own story and explain who you were before you knew Christ and who you are now and that Jesus is the difference between those two people.

Third, there may be someone at your work who is struggling with their faith and needs to see what it looks like for someone to stand up for Christ. You may never know this about that person. Or they may seek you out and thank you for doing what you did. Regardless, you may demonstrate to someone else what true followship of Jesus looks like. There also may be someone listening to you who has some rough times ahead of them. In those rough times, they will remember that you are a Christ-follower and they may seek you out for counsel.

It is for God's glory that you spoke out—let him now use it in people's lives, including yours. You can't beat yourself up about what you said or didn't say. Learn from it and get ready for the next opportunity. As Peter encourages us in 1 Peter 3:15, don't be forceful or disrespectful but be gracious, respect what people think (realize that they may not know any better and may be just verbalizing what they have been taught since they were a child), and be a source of wise truth for them—authentic in your words, compassionate for people, loving them with word and deed.

Keep growing through this—God is stretching you and it is very cool that you are growing through the stretching. Keep learning about God in his Word—learn about his character, his grace, his passion for people, and his compassion for the lost. Then through this learning, he will give you the knowledge to share about himself. Typically when people are living apart from God, it is because they either have a wrong understanding of God (e.g., that he is a policeman ready to beat them down, or a big Santa Claus who is an overweight jolly gift-giver, etc.), or they have a wrong perception of themselves (e.g., they think they are good enough on their own, or don't see inherent worth in their life). Try to show them the proper perspective on both of these issues through your words, your actions, and your decisions. Show them the love of God and make sure they know that they matter to you and to God. They will see that something is different about you in how you handle yourself, the decisions you make, and how you treat people. That difference will reflect the kingdom of God to them and that is the best thing you can ever do for them. It is not your job to save them, but to reveal the kingdom of God in their lives.

Regarding how they are making you feel, consider Psalm 56:4, 56:11, 118:6, and Hebrews 13:6 and the collective resolve of the writers to proclaim God as their helper, to not be afraid, and to recognize that the worst things that another human being could do to them aren't even that bad. One of the writers, David, was going through some tough times with people making life very difficult for him. They wanted to kill him for what he stood for—a rough situation to say the least. But even if they killed him, he knew that the next moment he would be with the Lord…not too bad upon reconsideration. So, consider what the worst thing is someone could do to you at work and then ask the same question David asked…what can they really do to me? Your confidence, security and identity are in Christ and him alone—rest in that.

Peace –
Kemper

Selected Scripture:

Study method:

Truth learned:

Steps I will take to apply it:

My message concerning "Leadership Development":

EPILOGUE

DEAR READER,
The final letter is one to you, written by Was Aarum, pastor of Vintage in Buffalo, NY where we serve. Enjoy his heart for you.

In this book, Kemper and Laura have talked a lot about relationships, purity, womanhood, and manhood. They have also discussed contentment, leadership, guilt, addiction, and freedom. Regardless of which issues you struggle with, the foundation of all human need is found in the person and work of Jesus Christ. It is in Jesus where we find purpose and it is in this purpose where we discover true, abundant, and eternal life. This life can begin today and can include pure relationships, authentic womanhood and manhood, joyful contentment, influential leadership, forgiveness of sin, and freedom from addictions. If you do not know Jesus personally, we would love to introduce you to him. Many people know about Jesus, much like they know about Michelangelo or William Shakespeare. But Jesus gives us the opportunity to be in a relationship with him. And in this relationship, we find salvation—the ability to know and experience God.

Thousands of years ago, King Solomon, inspired by God, wrote down this simple but profound truth, "He (God) has also set eternity in the human heart" (Ecclesiastes 3:11).

Though he was one of the wealthiest and wisest people to ever live, he discovered what you and I, if we're honest, know to be true as well—that the stuff of this world doesn't satisfy, doesn't bring lasting purpose, doesn't fill the void of meaning, and doesn't answer the heart's deepest questions in a person's life. The truth is it was never intended to. We are meant for something more. We are meant for a connection with the divine.

The Bible clearly maps this out in its very first book, Genesis. We as human beings from the beginning were created with a specific divine design. And that design is to be in a personal relationship with God, to know him and love him and live life as he designated it to be lived. However, this is not how things are. Our deconstruction began when sin entered the picture—man's rebellion against God, choosing to live life on his own terms. With sin, our disconnection from God is total, and the result is not only an aimless life apart from our Creator but an eternity separated from him as well. You and I are guilty of breaking God's law (see 1 John 3:4 and Exodus 20) and the consequences are dire (see John 3:36). But God does not end our story there, mired in hopelessness. His love for you and for me is so great that he launched a rescue mission, pursuing us with the possibility of a new life and the chance to be born again. Our desperate situation called for the most extreme of measures. The only way to satisfy and uphold the justice of a holy God was to pay for our eternal sin crime with a substitute who could completely and totally fulfill the death sentence leveled against us.

"For the wages of sin is death" (Romans 6:23). God sent the only qualified, acceptable "payment"—his Son Jesus—to earth to die in our place so that by believing in him and receiving by faith his sacrifice on our behalf, we become declared righteous (see Romans 1:16-17), we receive eternal life, a home in heaven (see 1

John 5:13), we are restored to our original design in a loving relationship with God through Jesus Christ (see 1 Peter 3:18 and 1 John 4:9-10), and the eternal void of meaning in our life is filled (see John 10:10). The way this truth can become a reality in your life today is through faith—believing that what God says in his Word, the Bible, is for real, and then by coming to God on his terms: agreeing with God that you have broken his law and are guilty of sin (Romans 3:23—"For all have sinned…"), accepting Jesus' death sacrifice for you as the only way to get to God (John 14:6—"Jesus said, 'I am the way, the truth and the life. No one comes to the Father but by me.'"), willfully turning from sin and living life on your own terms—the Bible calls this "repentance" (Luke 13:3—"I tell you the truth, unless you repent you shall all likewise perish"), and by turning to Jesus and placing your faith in him (John 1:12—"Yet to all who received him, to those who believed in his name, he gave the right to become children of God").

Right now, right where you are at, you can voice your heart's desire to Jesus through prayer and commit your life to him. And that is exactly what it is—a life commitment, responding to God who is desperately pursuing you as the great lover of your soul. For God to ask for a lesser commitment would not only cheapen it but would also be completely unsatisfactory in dealing with our spiritual condition. We don't just need a spiritual Band-Aid, we need a total life transfusion. It is this that God offers us (see John 17:3), wrapping it up in an ongoing, purpose-driven, outrageous love relationship with himself. And it's one you can be confident in forever (see 1 John 5:11-13). This is where the journey begins, and God leaves the invitation open to you. It is the only answer to the call of eternity in your heart.

You can form your prayer like this (There's no magic formula in the words of the prayer. What matters is that you express what you now realize in your heart before God.):

"Dear God, I believe that you are telling me the truth in your Word, and I agree with it. I confess that I am a sinner, and I need to be rescued. I need a savior. I believe that you sent your Son, Jesus, to die on a cross to pay the penalty for my sin. I believe that he rose from the grave, conquering sin and death, and now offers me eternal life—a relationship with you forever. I want that. So right now, Jesus, I turn from my sin in repentance and I turn to you. Come into my life, forgive my sin, and give me eternal life. I commit my life to you. Thank you for becoming my Savior, my friend, my Lord. I love you. Thank you for loving me. Guide me now, please, as I follow you. Amen."

Being a Christ-follower is all about relationship—living, growing and enjoying a love relationship with Jesus Christ. That's his desire and his plan for you. His love for you is unlike anything else you'll ever experience—perfect, complete, consistent, eternal (check out these verses: John 14:23, 15:9-10; Romans 8:31-39).

Daily connect with Jesus and grow in your love relationship with him. Pray, read the Bible, and live out the truths that God is teaching you from his Word.

We are so excited about what God is doing in your life! If you would like to connect with us at Vintage, or if you would like additional resources to help you grow in your relationship to Christ, please visit our website at www.vintagetruth.com.

Thank you for the privilege of sharing God's Word with you. No kidding, it really is an honor.

Wes Aarum
Pastor of Vintage
The Chapel at CrossPoint
Buffalo, NY USA
www.vintagetruth.com

AFTERWORD

WE CAN'T HELP but wonder where you are now, and what day it is in your life that has brought you to this page, this book's ending, that could be—we hope—a new beginning for you. We're wondering what God has taught you about himself that is now forever a part of you. And we can't help but wonder: *What will you do with those lessons?* Who will you include in this eternal message between men and women of God? After all a truly great message is one worth inviting others to live with you.

> And for us this is the end of all the stories, and we can most truly say that they all lived happily ever after. But for them it was only the beginning of the real story. All their life in this world and all their adventures in Narnia had only been the cover and the title page: now at last they were beginning Chapter One of the Great Story, which no one on earth has read, which goes on forever: in which every chapter is better than the one before.
>
> C.S. Lewis, *The Last Battle*

WORKS CITED

Arthur, Kay. *How to Study the Bible*. Eugene: Harvest House Publishers, 1994.

Gillis, Jerry. *Followship: The Essence of Our Journey with Jesus*. Mustang: Tate Publishing, 2005.

Kendall, Jackie, and Jones Debby. *Lady in Waiting: Becoming God's Best While Waiting for Mr. Right*. Shippensburg: Destiny Image Publishers, Inc., 1995.

Lewis, C.S. *The Last Battle*. Collier Books: New York, 1978.

Mayhew, Billy. "It's a Sin to Tell a Lie." *Live at the Sydney Opera House*, Recorded 1978. RCA Victor 1999. compact disc

Stanley, Andy. *The Best Question Ever*. Colorado Springs: Multnomah Publishers, 2004.

Thomas, Angela. *Do You Think I'm Beautiful?* Nashville: Thomas Nelson, 2005.